DATE DUE

Olympism

A BASIC GUIDE TO THE HISTORY, IDEALS, AND SPORTS OF THE OLYMPIC MOVEMENT

An Official U.S. Olympic Committee Sports Series

The U.S. Olympic Committee

Griffin Publishing Group

This Hardcover Edition Distributed By
Gareth Stevens Publishing
A World Almanac Education Group Company

This hardcover edition distributed by
Gareth Stevens Publishing
A World Almanac Education Group Company
330 West Olive Street, Suite 100
Milwaukee, WI 53212 USA

For a free color catalog describing Gareth Stevens' list of high-quality books and multimedia programs, call 1-800-542-2595 (USA) or 1-800-461-9120 (Canada). Gareth Stevens Publishing's Fax: (414) 332-3567.
Visit Gareth Stevens' website at: www.garethstevens.com

Library of Congress Cataloging-in-Publication Data for this hardcover edition available upon request from Gareth Stevens Publishing. Fax: (414) 336-0157 for the attention of the Publishing Records Department.

Hardcover edition: ISBN 0-8368-2800-3

Editorial Statement
In the interest of brevity, the Editors have chosen to use the standard English form of address. Please be advised that this usage is not meant to suggest a restriction to, nor an endorsement of, any individual or group of individuals, either by age, gender, or athletic ability. The Editors certainly acknowledge that boys and girls, men and women, of every age and physical condition are actively involved in sports, and we encourage everyone to enjoy the sports of his or her choice.

1 2 3 4 5 6 7 8 9 05 04 03 02 01
Printed in the United States of America

ACKNOWLEDGMENTS

PUBLISHER	**Griffin Publishing Group**
DIR. / OPERATIONS	**Robin L. Howland**
PROJECT MANAGER	**Bryan K. Howland**
WRITER	**Suzanne Ledeboer**
BOOK DESIGN	**m2design group**

USOC	
CHAIRMAN/PRESIDENT	**William J. Hybl**

EDITORS	**Geoffrey M. Horn**
	Catherine Gardner
PHOTOS	**Lisa Davis**
	The Olympic Challenge 1988
COVER DESIGN	**m2design group**
COVER PHOTO	**The Sporting Image/Eileen Langsley**

The United States Olympic Committee

The U.S. Olympic Committee (USOC) is the custodian of the U.S. Olympic Movement and is dedicated to providing opportunities for American athletes of all ages.

The USOC, a streamlined organization of member organizations, is the moving force for support of sports in the United States that are on the program of the Olympic and/or Pan American Games, or those wishing to be included.

The USOC has been recognized by the International Olympic Committee since 1894 as the sole agency in the United States whose mission involves training, entering, and underwriting the full expenses for the United States teams in the Olympic and Pan American Games. The USOC also supports the bid of U.S. cities to host the winter and summer Olympic Games, or the winter and summer Pan American Games, and after reviewing all the candidates, votes on and may endorse one city per event as the U.S. bid city. The USOC also approves the U.S. trial sites for the Olympic and Pan American Games team selections.

WELCOME TO THE OLYMPIC SPORTS SERIES

We feel this unique series will encourage parents, athletes of all ages, and novices who are thinking about a sport for the first time to get involved with the challenging and rewarding world of Olympic sports.

This series of Olympic sport books covers both summer and winter sports, features Olympic history and basic sports fundamentals, and encourages family involvement. Each book includes information on how to get started in a particular sport, including equipment and clothing; rules of the game; health and fitness; basic first aid; and guidelines for spectators. Of special interest is the information on opportunities for senior citizens, volunteers, and physically challenged athletes. In addition, each book is enhanced by photographs and illustrations and a complete, easy-to-understand glossary.

Because this family-oriented series neither assumes nor requires prior knowledge of a particular sport, it can be enjoyed by all age groups. Regardless of anyone's level of sports knowledge, playing experience, or athletic ability, this official U.S. Olympic Committee Sports Series will encourage understanding and participation in sports and fitness.

The purchase of these books will assist the U.S. Olympic Team. This series supports the Olympic mission and serves importantly to enhance participation in the Olympic and Pan American Games.

United States Olympic Committee

Contents

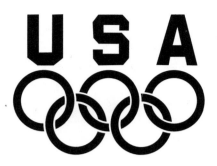

AN ATHLETE'S CREED

The most important thing in the Olympic Games is not to win but to take part, just as the most important thing in life is not the triumph but the struggle. The essential thing is not to have conquered but to have fought well.

These famous words, commonly referred to as the Olympic Creed, were once spoken by Baron Pierre de Coubertin, founder of the modern Olympic Games. Whatever their origins, they aptly describe the theme behind each and every Olympic competition.

Metric Equivalents

Wherever possible, measurements given are those specified by the Olympic rules. Other measurements are given in metric or standard U.S. units, as appropriate. For purposes of comparison, the following rough equivalents may be used.

1 kilometer (km)	= 0.62 mile (mi)	1 mi = 1.61 km
1 meter (m)	= 3.28 feet (ft)	1 ft = 0.305 m
	= 1.09 yards (yd)	1 yd = 0.91 m
1 centimeter (cm)	= 0.39 inch (in)	1 in = 2.54 cm
	= 0.1 hand	1 hand (4 in) = 10.2 cm
1 kilogram (kg)	= 2.2 pounds (lb)	1 lb = 0.45 kg
1 milliliter (ml)	= 0.03 fluid ounce (fl oz)	1 fl oz = 29.573 ml
1 liter	= 0.26 gallons (gal)	1 gal = 3.785 liters

1

What Is Olympism?

Olympism is an idea, or concept, with roots reaching all the way back to ancient Greece. It contains certain fundamental goals or objectives for the education of individuals.

The Ancient View

Ancient Greek philosophers believed that all young men should engage in physical exercise to develop a strong, healthy body. Also, they believed that a strong, healthy individual needed to practice moral and spiritual virtues.

At the sacred complex of Epidauros, two marble columns at the entrance to the Temple of Asclepius, the god of healing and medicine, bear this admonition:

> Pure must be he who enters the fragrant temple;
> Purity means to think nothing but holy thoughts.

The design of such sacred sites as Epidauros, Delphi, and Olympia expressed the ancient Greeks' belief that body, mind, and spirit were inseparable aspects of the whole person. There were the stadium and gymnasium, where athletes' physical performance was put to the test. Close-by temples served the contestants' spiritual needs for pure thought and visualization. At the vast amphitheater, drama and music evoked the audience's emotional responses of rhythm and harmony. This concept of the "whole person" was echoed by the Roman poet Juvenal, *"A healthy mind in a healthy body."*

The Greeks' recognition that the care of mind and spirit were integral to athletic performance was an important part of the Olympic tradition. However, only in recent years did sports psychology and mental training in imagination reintroduce the view that mental and psychological attitudes were an important aspect of physical performance. Attention to the mental and psychological side of sports seems to have been first championed in the former U.S.S.R. and satellite countries. And so we are no longer surprised by the statement that "the more man's thought communes with the divine harmony, the more spiritual, powerful, and healthy he becomes," made by modern Greek anthropologist Theodore Papadakis, reflecting once more the spirit of ancient Olympism.

A Modern Definition

A more modern definition, applied to today's world, might be as follows:

- *Olympism* promotes self-development and improvement of the individual, man or woman, by emphasizing and valuing the qualities of:

    —Self-discipline

    —Courage

    —Perseverance

    —Self-direction

    —Self-esteem

    —Personal fitness

- *Olympism* nurtures these qualities through lifelong participation in exercise and sport.

- *Olympism* holds these qualities to be essential, not just in games, but in life in general.

- *Olympism* fosters high levels of human interaction:

  —Sportsmanship and fair play

  —Respect for one's opponents

  —Teamwork and cooperation

  —Friendly competition

  —International goodwill

- *Olympism* applies to all levels of sport—from novice to Olympic champion.

- *Olympism* relates to the conduct of:

  —Athletes and coaches

  —Officials and trainers

  —Sport administrators

  —Teachers and school administrators

  —Spectators and general public

  —Representatives of the media

Olympism, according to this view, is a strong moral force that seeks and promotes:

  —Individual well-being

  —National spirit

  —International understanding and friendship

One Example of the Spirit of Olympism

The spirit of modern Olympism has been reflected by many individuals. One who did so was Clifton Cushman, a renowned track star at the University of Kansas. He had won the intermediate hurdles three times at the Kansas Relay and the silver medal in the 400-meter hurdles at the 1960 Rome Olympic Games. During the U.S. Olympic Trials, he was leading the race to qualify for the 1964 Olympic team when he stumbled on the last hurdle and fell—failing to qualify for a chance to win the gold medal.

Many people, including the students at his high school, wrote telling him how sorry they felt about his unfortunate tumble. To the students he sent back the following letter—

An Open Letter to Young People

Don't feel sorry for me. I feel sorry for some of you! [You may have seen me on TV] hit the fifth hurdle, fall and lie on the track in an inglorious heap of skinned elbows, bruised hips, torn knees, and injured pride, unsuccessful in my attempt to make the Olympic team .... In a split second all the many years of training, pain, sweat, blisters and agony of running were ... wiped out. But I tried! I would much rather fail knowing I had put forth an honest effort than never to have tried at all.

Let me tell you something about yourselves .... You are spending more money, enjoying more freedom, and driving more cars than ever before, yet many of you are very unhappy. Some of you have never known the satisfaction of doing your best in sports, the joy of excelling in class, the wonderful feeling of completing a job, any job, and looking back on it knowing that you have done your best.

I dare you [to do what you know is right] and not wilt under the comments of your so-called friends. I dare you to clean up your language. I dare you to honor your mother and father. I dare you to go to church without having to be compelled to go .... I dare you to unselfishly help someone less fortunate than yourself and enjoy the wonderful feeling that goes with it. I dare you to become physically fit. I dare you to read a book that is not required in school. I dare you to look up at the stars, not down at the mud, and set your sights on one of them that, up to now, you thought was unattainable. There is plenty of room at the top, but no room for anyone to sit down.

Clifton E. Cushman

A well-known symbol of the ancient Olympic Games,
The Discus Thrower

2

The Olympics in Ancient Greece

When and where the ancient games began has been lost in the distant past. Most young people do seem to have a built-in desire to test their physical strength and skill—usually in some type of contest. The earliest records that we have indicate that almost every ancient society had some form of organized athletic activity. The ancient civilizations of Egypt and China, as well as the first Native Americans, had organized sports events.

The Olympic Games gained their name from their birthplace, the small Greek city of Olympia in the small "kingdom" of Elis. The first record we have of an Olympic Game being held is in the year 776 B.C. The first recorded champion was a fellow by the name of Coroebus, a cook, who lived in Elis. He had won the sprint from one end of the stadium to the other—one "stade" or about 180 meters (about 600 feet).

The Greeks later dated their calendar by this event. They also began keeping records of Olympic winners, often erecting statues to honor the most famous of champions. Finally, the Greeks began charting their history by Olympiads—the four-year cycle between the Games—a practice that would continue uninterrupted for more than a thousand years.

Ancient Greece

The earliest sporting activity at Olympia, as elsewhere in Greece, was a mixture of athleticism, religion, education, culture, and the arts. The contestants were local men from the surrounding cities and villages who came to the festivals to honor the gods and test themselves.

> The ancient Greeks idealized clarity of mind and youthful vigor. They believed that man's physical prowess and athletic skills should be honored along with the capability of his mind. Thus, it was natural to combine athletic contests and religious ceremonies in the great festivals.
>
> *The Olympic Challenge 1988*

At the first thirteen Games, or festivals, the only athletic event was the "Dromos"—a fast-paced dash from one end of the Olympic stadium to the other. The distance was about 180 meters, and came to be known as one "stade" or stadium. (When additional races were later added, they were usually multiples of this distance—360 meters, etc.)

The Ideals of the Ancient Olympics

Combining worship and games made sense to the ancient Greeks because, while they asked the help of the gods to improve their lives, they also knew that *they* must be persevering, hard-working, and self-reliant in order to be successful. From these efforts came pride in their endeavors and a sense of personal accomplishment.

> There is no greater glory for a man as long as he lives than that which he wins by his own hands and feet.
>
> Homer, *The Odyssey*

Since the Greeks sought to emphasize their most important values—truth and beauty—early Olympic festivals also included music, dance, and art, as well as sports. These festivals celebrated the involvement of the whole person—the well-rounded individual. As such, ancient Olympism embodied the Greek idea of *kalos kagathos*, the harmonious development of the individual—physically, intellectually, and spiritually.

Victory in the early Games was considered important, but only when earned through courageous, dignified, and graceful action. *How* an athlete won was as important as winning.

As the Games took on a greater significance, marble and stone were used to build temples. The first temple honored the goddess Hera. Later, a great temple dedicated to Zeus—the most powerful of Greek gods—was constructed with 60-foot pillars. Within it was a 40-foot-tall gold and ivory statue of Zeus inlaid with jewels; in his right hand was a statue of Nike (Victory), and in his left was a scepter on which an eagle perched. Its beauty caused it to be called one of the seven wonders of the ancient world.

The temple and sacrificial altar of Zeus at Olympia

The Rise of the Games

After the first dozen Games, the festival of Olympia came to include participants from more distant city-states. The Spartans, who emphasized the virtues of rigorous physical exercise, provided outstanding athletes and dominated the Games. As the Games became more prestigious, athletes from throughout the Greek world came to participate.

Nothing was more important to the Greeks than the Games, not even their unceasing warring among themselves. Moved by the spiritual context of the Games, King Iphitus of Elis, supported by other rulers and legislators, agreed to stop all fighting for the duration of the Olympic Festival. This cessation of hostilities became known as the Olympic Truce.

Different sporting events were gradually introduced to the Games, including such activities as jumping, throwing, wrestling, boxing, chariot racing, etc. Running events, also, were expanded to include races of different lengths, from the two-stade (360 meters) event to the longest race, known as the "dolichos" (equal to twenty-four stades). All of these were held within the stadium.

Chronology of New Events

776 B.C.	Single stade foot race
724 B.C.	Second foot race added—2 stades
720 B.C.	Endurance race of 4.5 kilometers added (about twelve times around the stadium)
699 B.C.	Boxing added
680 B.C.	Four-horse chariot race added
648 B.C.	Pancratium (combined boxing and wrestling added)
580 B.C.	Race in armor added

There were some twenty sporting events being contested by the sixth and fifth centuries B.C. The Olympic Games then were at the height of their glory. Most of the events were designed to test military skills and warrior stamina.

This was especially true of the armor race, in which contestants apparently carried a shield and wore a helmet and leg armor in making a double circuit of the stadium. There was a practical side to this exercise: it kept the young men physically fit for war.

A Typical Olympic Festival

In the spring of an Olympic year, three sacred heralds would set out from Olympia to visit every corner of the Greek world and announce the forthcoming games.

Each Greek city-state sent its best men, determined by local elimination trials. The winner would be decorated with a simple branch of wild olive, but the rewards were great in other ways.

The crowds idolized the great athletes, poets wrote odes to their triumphs, and sculptors immortalized them in bronze and marble. From the fifth century onward, monetary rewards also became associated with an Olympic championship.

The athletes were required to travel to Elis one month in advance of the games to train under the supervision of selected judges. The thousands of other participants—such as spectators, official representatives from many Greek cities, musicians, food and drink purveyors, etc.—could come when they chose.

Sitting in the scorching midsummer heat, the male audience would witness an extraordinary variety of activities. There were all of the sporting events—running, jumping, throwing, equestrian, and wrestling. In addition, there would be contests involving poetry, drama, and music.

The Marathon Legend

The most famous Greek-inspired race of all—the marathon of 42,195 meters, or 26 miles, 385 yards—was never a part of the Greek Olympics. The name comes from the legend of a Greek soldier who ran about 22 miles, from the Greek plains of Marathon to the city-state of Athens, to announce news of the great victory over the invading Persians. After making his important announcement, the courageous messenger was said to have dropped dead.

This story may be a myth, but its spirit of courage and sacrifice has provided inspiration to one of the most famous and popular running events of our time.

Women were barred from the stadium, even as spectators, because the male athletes performed naked and because it would have been unthinkable for women to perform likewise. Young girls could watch the events taking place inside the stadium, but the only woman in the stadium was the priestess of Demeter, the goddess of agriculture, who was required to watch the Games from the north side of the stadium.

Penalties for women who violated this prohibition were supposed to be harsh; however, there is no record of a severe penalty being administered. Apparently, only one woman, Kallipateira, daughter of Diagoras, was caught entering the stadium. She had trained her son Peisirodos in the skill of boxing and, on the day he fought in the Games, she slipped into the stadium disguised as a trainer. When her son won, she jumped over the barrier to embrace him and was recognized as a woman. The judges, because of her family's history of loyalty to the Games, were lenient and did not punish her. However, from then on, the trainers were required also to appear nude as were the contestants.

Outside the stadium, southwards towards the wide river valley, was the hippodrome where chariot races were held. Women were allowed in the hippodrome and were victors of some equestrian events, as Olympic championships were awarded to the owners of the horses.

The Opening Day's Events

At Olympia, the chariot race was the opening event, but only after a previous day of preparation and worship. The two-wheeled chariots, each drawn by four horses abreast, entered the stadium in a ceremonial procession led by judges dressed in purple robes, a herald, and a trumpeter. As each chariot passed in front of the judges' stand, the herald would call out the names of the owner, his father, and his city. Then he would proclaim that the games were officially open.

The number of chariots varied, up to forty-one at the Pythian Games in 462 B.C. A large field made for an exciting contest because they all would start together and rush toward the turning post some 400 meters away. The trumpeter would signal the start, and the chariots would make twelve circuits, more than 9 kilometers, around the turning post.

An ancient Olympic chariot race on a piece of classical Greek pottery

Chariot races were very dangerous and required the most skillful of drivers. Collisions were common on the narrow course, and it was not uncommon for only one chariot to complete the race. Not unlike modern times, it was the accidents that provided most of the thrills for the crowd.

The Second Day's Events

The pentathlon was held during the afternoon of the second day. The athletes had to participate in five events—the discus, long jump, javelin, 200-meter sprint, and wrestling. All events except the final event, wrestling, were held in the stadium, while the wrestling took place in an open area near the altar of Zeus.

The number of entrants in the pentathlon was usually small, and it was not uncommon for some to drop out along the way, while others were eliminated by their performances. Victory was not calculated by points. If anyone was first in three events, he was declared the winner and the contest ended. Otherwise, the field was reduced for the final contest, the wrestling, to those competitors who still had a chance to win because of their placement in the four completed events.

Usually it was a head-to-head bout between two finalists that decided the overall pentathlon winner.

The Third Day's Events

The third day of competition was scheduled to coincide with the second or third full moon after the summer solstice. The morning was again dominated with religious activities. Varied religious rites, private and public, were followed by a great procession that began at the magistrate's house and wound its way to the altar of Zeus. The parade included judges, priests, the representatives from the cities, athletes, friends, and trainers. Arriving at the altar, they watched the slaying of 100 oxen. The roasted meat was taken to the magistrate's house where it was consumed at a gala banquet.

During the afternoon, three events for boys were held—the 200-meter race, wrestling, and boxing. A "boy" was defined as a young male between the ages of twelve and seventeen. This rather loose definition in a society without birth certificates created some problems, but not enough to cause the creation of classes of boys, as was done in other Greek games.

The Final Day's Events

The morning of the final day was occupied with three running events—200 meters, 400 meters, and the long-distance race ("dolichos") of 4,800 meters. The 200-meter sprint was simply a full dash across the stadium, but the historical accounts of the longer runs have left us with some unanswered questions. Was there one turning pole for runners, or separate turning poles for each athlete? There were rules against tripping and bumping, but ancient writers suggest that such tricks were frequent.

Because they were run on the same day, only a truly extraordinary athlete could win all three sprinting events at the same Games. Such an individual would be called a tripler.

The greatest Olympic runner was Leonidas of Rhodes, who won all three events at four consecutive festivals spanning twelve years between 164 and 152 B.C. Another outstanding competitor was Polites of Keramos, who won the two short sprints and the dolichos in the same day.

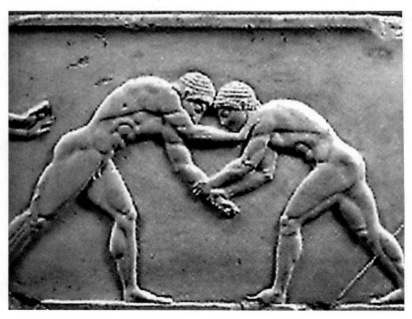

Wrestlers

Finally, on the last afternoon came the rough but popular body contact sports: boxing, wrestling, and pancratium—a combination of wrestling and judo, with a bit of boxing thrown in. The procedure was simple. Names were drawn from a silver urn, setting up initial matches and creating the pairing of matches that would lead to the final or championship bouts. All three sports were brutal, with few rules, no time limits, and no ring. There were also no weight classes so the competition was limited to big, tough, well-muscled men.

The objective in wrestling was to score three falls, a fall being defined as touching the ground with the knees. Milo of Croton was one of the most famous of the legendary strongmen who won this popular event. He is said to have developed his great strength by carrying a calf around every day, and as the calf grew into a large bull, he would be carrying each day a heavier weight. There may have been some truth to this story, for Milo won the boys' wrestling in 540 B.C. and the senior event at five successive Games.

Presumably biting or gouging was prohibited, but not much else was. A fifth century B.C. wrestler named Leonticus, from Messina in Sicily, tried to break his opponent's fingers as quickly as possible. He was remembered as one of the first wrestlers to develop new "holds."

Boxing, however, was even more brutal than wrestling. Leather thongs were wound tightly around the hands and wrists, leaving the fingers free. Blows were allowed with the fist and hand. The two contestants fought on without break until one or the other was knocked out or raised his hand as a sign of

The pancratium, a combination of wrestling, judo, and boxing

defeat. Violent activity was what attracted the spectators and that was what they saw.

The final pugilistic event in the afternoon of the fourth day was the pancratium. The contestants punched, slapped, kicked, wrestled, and, though illegal, would bite and gouge each other until one surrendered by tapping the victor on the back or shoulder.

One more event remained before the competition was closed, the 400-meter race in armor. Some writers say that it was held last to mark the end of the truce that was struck for each of the Games by warring states. The simpler and more plausible explanation is that it was felt desirable to reflect in the Games the fact that the infantry had supplanted the cavalry as the main Greek military unit.

The Expansion of Athletics

Athletics reached a peak of popularity between the sixth and fifth centuries B.C. Almost 200 years after the first recorded festival at Olympia, other major sports festivals were established. The Pythian Games in honor of the god Apollo were begun at Delphi in 582 B.C. The Isthmian Games were begun near Corinth the same year, held in honor of the god Poseidon. With the addition of the Nemean Games, the fourth major festival was founded.

Not surprisingly, the greatest ambition of the Greek athlete was to win a championship at each of the Games. As the competition became more intense, the participants gradually changed. The first Olympic Games were dominated by the part-time, occasional local athletes from nearby villages, but as these Games began to grow in popularity they became dominated by young men of wealth who had the resources to hire the best coaches and the time to train.

As the sports circuit expanded, many of the athletes became professionals who lived off the rewards bestowed by the state and aristocracy. These young men trained year-round and traveled from festival to festival, including the Olympic Games, to compete with one another for the increasingly larger prizes.

Among the major sports festivals, only the Olympic Games did not offer cash prizes. The glory of becoming an Olympic champion had a great many rewards—being honored in song, story, and victory parades. There were financial rewards as well, given by grateful cities and local wealthy sportsmen. When Olympic champions retired, they could usually count on ample pensions to support them the rest of their lives.

The Olympics continued to be bound by tradition and to be governed conservatively. One example of this conservatism relates to women. For centuries, Greek schoolgirls wearing tunics competed in sports contests. Traditionally, women had been restricted to contests of their own during special festivals. Later, with the increasing emancipation of women, especially in the cities, other short-distance races were introduced for girls and young women at many of the games and festivals.

At Olympia, for example, there was a race in honor of Zeus' consort Hera. The "Heraea" was marked out on only two-thirds of the stadium, some 160 meters, for women contestants only. However, the Olympic Games resisted the addition of women's events. Indeed, women continued to be banned from the stadium even as spectators.

The Decline of the Games

The glory of the Olympic Games peaked at the height of classical Greek culture, some 250 years after the first recorded Games. Their decline was long and gradual, lasting some 950 years.

The first major blow to the Games came in 146 B.C. when they were moved to Rome after Greece was conquered and made part of the Roman Empire. Here the ideals of Olympia and the purity of the athletic contests became less important. As the

Games became entertainment spectacles, they took on unsavory overtones.

The stadium at Olympia today

Some athletes began accepting money from opponents in exchange for conceding victory, in spite of the threat of extensive penalties. The Emperor Nero, for example, arranged for several Olympic crowns to be awarded to him after forcing his opponents to withdraw.

In Rome, as profit and politics came to dominate competition, the Olympic Games lost their historic and religious origins.

The final blow to the Games came with the rise of early Christianity, which frowned upon glorification of the human body, viewed the celebration of Greek gods as a pagan ritual, and disliked the brutality and corruption of the Games. The Christian Emperor Theodosius I banned all pagan festivals, including the Games, in A.D. 393. However, they continued to be held until the ban was reissued and enforced by Justinian I in A.D. 529.

Photo: Lisa Davis

Delphi, one site of the ancient Games

The Rediscovery of Olympia

Olympia also had fallen upon desperate times. The destruction of its monuments began in A.D. 267, when many of the buildings were taken apart so that the stone could be used to build protective fortifications. One hundred and fifty years later, shortly after Emperor Theodosius' ban of all festivals at Olympia, the looting and destruction started.

The statue of Zeus is thought to have been taken to Constantinople, where it was later destroyed by fire. The great temples were torn apart by looters and toppled by two earthquakes in the sixth century A.D. Finally, spring floods of the river Alpheus slowly buried Olympia, covering one of the most honored and famous sites in the ancient world under a layer of mud and sand. It would remain forgotten for nearly a thousand years.

Europeans rediscovered the site of Olympia in the late 1700s; however, not until the first decade of the nineteenth century did

British archaeologists begin to visit the area. Serious efforts at unearthing and reconstructing the site, supervised by German archaeologists, began in 1874 under a contract with the Greek government. Soon the full magnificence of what had been Olympia was revealed to an excited world.

Students of the classics at European universities began speculating about the nature of the ancient Olympic Games. A few idealists even began to talk of their revival. One was Pierre de Coubertin.

3

The Rebirth of the Olympics & Olympism

There is nothing obscure about the origin of the modern Olympic Games. They owe their revival almost entirely to a French aristocrat, Baron Pierre de Coubertin. His single-minded, persistent efforts, which overcame many obstacles, led to the first modern Olympic Games held at Athens in 1896.

Coubertin's contributions to international athletics are to be found in three separate but related areas—the rebirth of the Olympic Games; a new emphasis on the Olympic ideals, which has been termed "Olympism"; and the Modern Olympic Movement.

Baron Pierre de Coubertin (1863-1937)

Coubertin was born in Paris on New Year's Day, 1863. He traced his ancestry to Louis IX and the powerful families of Normandy. Although physically frail as a young man, he participated in such sports as rowing, fencing, and boxing. He also read, traveled extensively, and developed his skills as a writer, philosopher, and educator. A determined idealist, an untiring reformer, and the author of thirty-six books, Coubertin came to believe that including physical exercise in his nation's educational program was vital.

Coubertin was inspired by the classical ideal of a sound body and mind, and the importance of physical training in building a strong nation and individual. He was moved to action by his dismay at the poor physical condition of his fellow Frenchmen, and the belief that this lack of fitness had led to France's humiliating defeat in the Franco-Prussian War of 1870-71. In the turbulent years that followed, France suffered low national esteem and a depressed economy, while the fortunes of England and Germany prospered.

Coubertin became convinced that it was the strength of the British education system and the role of sports in the private schools (called "public" schools in England) that were responsible for Britain's national power. He saw the schools, built on an elite educational system that developed a quality they termed "Muscular Christianity," as the foundation of Britain's political and military strength.

He visited several of these public schools where sports were a fundamental part of the curriculum, including the Rugby School, which was famous for graduating future British leaders. In 1890, he visited Shropshire, England, where he met Dr. W.P. Brookes who, in 1840, had established the Olympian Society and conducted an annual sports festival at a site called Olympia Fields. During his visit, Coubertin was made an honorary member of Dr. Brookes' Olympian Society. Popular sports fairs such as this had historical roots that reached back to medieval times.

These sports fairs, combined with Coubertin's enthusiastic fascination with ancient Greek philosophy and lifestyle, were key elements in the rebirth of the Olympic Games. Another major element was the public excitement about the archaeological findings at the legendary cities of Troy and Olympia, which led to a new fascination with ancient Greece throughout Europe.

Baron Pierre de Coubertin

Inspired and motivated, Coubertin began to write and lecture about the importance of physical education and the possible advantages of restoring the Olympic Games as an international event for promoting world peace. "Nothing in ancient history," he wrote, "has given me more food for thought than Olympia, this dream city."

Rebirth of the Olympic Games

In 1894, at an international meeting in Paris organized to study "amateurism," Coubertin succeeded in adding an item to the agenda: "[What is] the possibility of restoring the Olympic Games and under what conditions could they be restored?"

Coubertin proceeded to stage a dramatic presentation that included poetry, music, and songs. He concluded with a moving performance of the ancient "Hymn to Apollo," which recently had been discovered at Delphi. The awed and inspired seventy-nine delegates from twelve countries voted unanimously to restore the Games. At last, Baron de Coubertin had reason to believe that his long-sought goal was within reach. The newly appointed International Olympic Committee, consisting of fourteen members, agreed to try to launch the first modern Olympic Games in Athens during the spring of 1896.

When Coubertin initially sought to establish a local organizing group in Athens, he was met with a lack of interest and rejection. The Greek government was bankrupt, and lacking a national

Panathinakon Stadium in Athens, built for the 1896 Games

sports program, Athenians did not wish to see Greek athletes embarrassed. Persistence eventually won out, for Coubertin's idea finally gained the support of Crown Prince Constantine, who assisted the Frenchman in raising the funds to rebuild the ancient Athenian Games Stadium for the 1896 Games.

King George of Greece proclaimed the first modern Olympic Games open in Athens during the first week of April. The opening ceremony was witnessed by 70,000 enthusiastic spectators. There were 245 competitors, the majority of whom were Greeks, ready to begin the sports events. In all, thirteen countries were represented.

The start of the decathlon in the first modern Olympic Games

It was a modest beginning. The foreign athletes who came to Athens at their own expense were not the best athletes in their countries. The level of competition was further lessened because of technical factors: the track was extremely long and narrow, and the tight turns and soft surface of the 400-meter track hindered the runners. To make matters worse, they had to run in a clockwise direction—opposite to the standard direction of both then and now.

> The 1896 Games in Athens were more magnificent in their pomp and ceremony than in the brilliance of athletic performance. Yet, because no other event of such a multinational scope had been held, it was still a profound beginning.
>
> *The Olympic Challenge 1988*

When the competition got under way, U.S. athletes dominated the track events, the French prevailed in cycling, and the Swiss and Germans excelled in gymnastics. The Greeks had their share of victories—ten in all—in shooting and gymnastics events held at different locations in Athens.

As the final day dawned, however, the Greeks had not won in their own stadium. The impending disappointment of the hosts and their possible opposition to future Olympic Games evaporated when Spiridon Loues, a slight Greek peasant, trotted into the packed stadium on his way to victory in the first Olympic marathon run. (The "marathon" got its name from the fact it started in the town of Marathon and ended in Athens.) To the relief of organizers and hosts alike, the first Games were concluded on a popular note.

Spiridon Loues

The following tables list where subsequent Games were held and who participated.

The Olympic Summer Games

No.	Year	Host City	Nations	Events	Men	Women
I	1896	Athens, Greece	13	42	311	0
II	1900	Paris, France	22	60	1,319	11
III	1904	St. Louis, USA	12	67	681	6
IV	1908	London, England	23	104	1,999	36
V	1912	Stockholm, Sweden	28	106	2,490	57
VI	1916	Berlin, Germany	(canceled because of World War I)			
VII	1920	Antwerp, Belgium	27	154	2,543	64
VIII	1924	Paris, France	45	137	2,956	136
IX	1928	Amsterdam, Holland	46	120	2,724	290
X	1932	Los Angeles, USA	37	124	1,281	127
XI	1936	Berlin, Germany	49	142	3,738	328
XII	1940	Tokyo, Japan & Helsinki, Finland*	(canceled because of World War II)			
XIII	1944	London, England	(canceled because of World War II)			
XIV	1948	London, England	59	138	3,714	385
XV	1952	Helsinki, Finland	69	149	4,407	518
XVI	1956	Melbourne, Australia & Stockholm, Sweden*	67 29	145 6	2,958 145	384 13
XVII	1960	Rome, Italy	84	150	4,738	610
XVIII	1964	Tokyo, Japan	94	162	4,457	683
XIX	1968	Mexico City, Mexico	113	172	4,750	781
XX	1972	Munich, Germany	122	196	5,848	1,300
XXI	1976	Montreal, Canada	92	199	4,834	1,274
XXII	1980	Moscow, USSR	81	200	4,265	1,192
XXIII	1984	Los Angeles, USA	140	223	5,458	1,620
XXIV	1988	Seoul, Korea	160	237	6,983	2,438
XXV	1992	Barcelona, Spain	171	257	7,555	3,008
XXVI	1996	Atlanta, USA	197	275	6,472	4,316
XXVII	2000	Sydney, Australia		300		
XXVIII	2004	Athens, Greece				

* equestrian events
Source: *IOC Official Olympic Companion, Atlanta 1996 Official Commemorative Book.*

The Olympic Winter Games

No.	Year	Host City	Nations	Events	Men	Women
I	1924	Chamonix, France	16	13	281	13
II	1928	St. Moritz, Switzerland	25	13	366	27
III	1932	Lake Placid, USA	17	14	277	30
IV	1936	Garmisch-Partenkirchen, Germany	28	17	680	76
		(Games for 1940 & 1944 were canceled due to World War II)				
V	1948	St. Moritz, Switzerland	28	24	636	77
VI	1952	Oslo, Norway	30	22	624	108
VII	1956	Cortina d'Ampezzo Italy	32	24	687	132
VIII	1960	Squaw Valley, USA	30	27	502	146
IX	1964	Innsbruck, Austria	36	34	758	175
X	1968	Grenoble, France	37	35	1,063	230
XI	1972	Sapporo, Japan	35	35	927	218
XII	1976	Innsbruck, Austria	37	37	1,013	248
XIII	1980	Lake Placid, USA	37	39	1,012	271
XIV	1984	Sarajevo, Yugoslavia	49	40	1,127	283
XV	1988	Calgary, Canada	57	46	1,270	364
XVI	1992	Albertville, France	64	57	1,801	488
XVII	1994*	Lillehammer, Norway	67	61	1,302	542
XVIII	1998	Nagano, Japan	80	68	1,389	788
XVIV	2002	Salt Lake City, USA				

* Began alternating with the Summer Games so that there would be Olympic Games every two years.

Source: *1995 Olympic Fact Book*, USOC/*Golden Book of Olympics*, 1992; there are some discrepancies between the two sets of figures.

The preceding tables show just how "international" the Games have become. They also reflect the growing number of events and the increasing number of participants, especially women.

The success of the modern Games, however, has not been without controversies and disappointments. There have arisen a number of issues which the International Olympic Committee and the National Olympic Committees have had to face.

War and Politics

While ancient Greek wars between city-states actually stopped while the Games were in progress, such has not been the case in the modern era. World War I resulted in the cancellation of the 1916 Games, and World War II forced the cancellation of the 1940 and 1944 Games. Even though the war had been over for three years, the Japanese, German, and Italian athletes were excluded from the 1948 Olympic Games because their countries were charged with starting World War II.

International politics also has resulted in the exclusion of athletes from the Games. Beginning in 1968, South African athletes were excluded from the Games because that country practiced discrimination (apartheid) against its Black citizens. With a dramatic change in its national racial policy, South African athletes were allowed to reenter the Games in 1992.

The most violent interjection of politics into the Olympics occurred during the 1972 Summer Games. Eleven members of the Israeli team were seized in their Olympic quarters by Arab terrorists. Two were killed almost immediately, and the other nine were murdered after being held hostage. In 1995, a 33-foot-long granite memorial, engraved with the victims' likenesses and names, was dedicated at Munich, Germany.

The politics of the "Cold War"—between the United States and its allies and the Soviet Union and its allies—influenced the Olympic Games from 1952 to 1988. As each of the Games was held, the media perhaps focused undue attention on the "battle" of the medal count—constantly emphasizing which nation, the United States or the U.S.S.R., won the most gold, silver, and bronze medals. In this way, the Games often overshadowed the athletes as, unfortunately, the Games were viewed as contests between political systems—democracy and communism.

In 1976 and 1980, athletes from Taiwan, who had previously represented non-communist or "nationalist" China, could not compete in the Games under the flag of China. Instead, athletes from the People's Republic of China were recognized as the official representatives of their nation, while the Taiwanese were allowed to compete under the Olympic flag.

In 1980, the United States led thirty-five other countries in a boycott of that year's Olympic Games held in Moscow. These nations refused to participate in the Games because the Soviet Union sent its soldiers into Afghanistan. In retaliation, the Soviet Union and some of its allied nations boycotted the 1984 Olympic Games in Los Angeles.

By 1992, the Cold War had ended. Russia and a series of new republics now replaced the Soviet Union's communist government. Since each of the new republics could not afford to send individual teams, the former Soviet Olympic athletes were allowed to compete as the "Unified Team" using the Olympic flag and the Olympic Hymn in place of national flags and anthems.

Redefining Amateurism

When the modern Olympics began in 1896, Baron de Coubertin had insisted that a major reason for the Games was to "teach that sport is played for fun and enjoyment and not to make money ... the philosophy of amateurism as contrasted to that of materialism." This notion of amateurism—sport as an activity gentlemen of means played—dominated the early years of the modern Games.

The elitist definition of amateur status was reflected in the decision to strip Native American Jim Thorpe—often called the United States' greatest all-round male athlete—of the two gold medals he won in the pentathlon and decathlon at the 1912 Stockholm Games. In 1913, he returned the medals after he was disqualified for having violated the amateur status regulations for playing semiprofessional baseball during two summers. The Thorpe family and others continued to protest the IOC's disqualification.

In 1982, the International Olympic Committee sought to make amends by reinstating Thorpe as winner of the 1912 decathlon and pentathlon. Subsequently, IOC president Juan Antonio Samaranch invited all living members of the Thorpe family to Lausanne, Switzerland, and presented Jim Thorpe's son Carl with copies of the original gold medals.

Jim Thorpe

In the years after World War II, the definition of who were "amateur" athletes became a matter of serious debate. In part because of the impact of Cold War politics, some nations began providing financial support to their athletes. Often athletes were assigned a military rank, which provided a salary and living expenses, while they spent their time in training and competition. Still other countries began screening their children at a young age and selecting those with unusual athletic abilities for intensive training for Olympic competition.

For years U.S. Olympic athletes argued that they were at a disadvantage. Often U.S. amateur athletes had to support themselves at jobs that greatly limited their training time and competitive opportunities.

Gradually the term "eligible athlete" replaced "amateur" and it became the responsibility of each International Federation to establish the rules of eligibility for its sport. Within these guidelines, U.S. athletes began to receive financial support in the form of prize money, trust funds, direct cash payments, and "tailored" jobs. Obviously, the more popular sports attracted much more financial support than the lesser-known ones.

At the Barcelona Games in 1992, the first group of highly-paid professional U.S. athletes—the "Dream Team"—easily won the basketball gold medal.

Finances and Commercialism

The popular success of the modern Olympic Games has come in large part from the advent of television. Millions of people, far beyond the various sport sites, now can watch the Games in their living rooms with a view of the activities as good as or, oftentimes, better than those attending the Games.

As the number of events and participants has increased, so have the costs of conducting the Games. The funds to meet these costs, together with additional millions of dollars used by the IOC to finance a wide variety of programs and sports groups, have been raised from commercial sponsors. Individuals seeking the means to expand IOC activities argue that even more aggressive efforts should be made to achieve more sponsorships.

Many of the people who support the Olympic Movement, whether as coaches, competitors, or spectators, are beginning to worry that overcommercialization may, at some point, prompt the public to turn away from the Games. After all, there is the example of the downfall of the ancient Games due in large measure to "overcommercialization."

These critics argue that commercialization of the Games raises a number of questions as to legitimacy and control. The IOC used to do a good job of keeping advertising out of the stadiums; however, it has not been nearly so successful recently, with advertisers desiring to reach the huge television audiences.

According to critics such as Bruce Kidd, the Modern Olympic Movement must confront such difficult questions as—

- What principles should govern the Olympic Movement's various partnerships with governments and corporations?

- How can the Olympic Movement ensure that the Olympic ideals and meanings are effectively conveyed in all sponsorships, including those with television?

- How can we protect and strengthen athletes' and coaches' rights of individual expression against the massive power of governments and the corporations?

Finding answers to these and other vital questions will determine the future success of the Olympic Games.

*Goals of the Olympic Games**

The Olympic Games ... were not revived by Baron de Coubertin merely to give contestants a chance to win medals and to break records, nor to entertain the public, nor to provide for the participants a stepping stone to a career in professional sport, nor certainly to demonstrate the superiority of one political system over another. His idea was that they would—

(1) Bring to the attention of the world the fact that national programs of physical training and competitive sport will not only develop stronger and healthier boys and girls, but also, and perhaps more important, will make better and happier citizens through the character building that follows participation in properly administered amateur sport.

(2) Demonstrate the principles of fair play and good sportsmanship, which could be adopted with great advantage in many other spheres of activity.

(3) Stimulate interest in the fine arts through exhibitions, concerts, and demonstrations during the Game period and thus contribute to broader and more well-rounded life.

(4) Teach that sport is played for fun and enjoyment and not to make money, and that with devotion to the task at hand, the reward will take care of itself—the philosophy of "amateurism" as contrasted to that of "professionalism."

(5) Create international friendship and good will, thus leading to a happier and more peaceful world.

* The International Olympic Academy, *Introduction to the History, Philosophy and Actual Situation of the Olympic Games and Movement* (Ancient Olympia, Greece).

The Modern Olympic Movement

The Modern Olympic Movement, which gained guidance and direction from Baron de Coubertin, refers to activities and programs of various organizations to achieve worldwide reaffirmation of ideals and values which are reflected in the legacy of the Olympic Games. This network extends from the International Olympic Committee, to the International Sports Federations, to the National Olympic Committees, to local groups who sponsor athletic events.

The Olympic Movement seeks to inform people of the educational benefits of combining sports and physical activities with artistic and intellectual endeavors. It encourages more and more individuals to participate in all of these activities at levels of intensity and competition that are appropriate to them.

While Coubertin wanted to improve the health and strength of young people, more importantly he desired to guide them toward becoming better citizens, more honest and efficient, with an optimistic and pleasant disposition and a stronger personality. "That which is most important in the lives of modern people [is] education," Coubertin wrote a century ago after visiting the United States and Canada.

Sport, Coubertin believed, would provide an essential moral part of education: "If it develops muscles, it also forms character and will ... Sport seeks out fear to dominate it, exhaustion to triumph over it."

The emphasis on "sustained effort" is at the heart of Olympic philosophy. The constant and almost unquenchable desire to strive for something better is a basic part of success. The competitive spirit is noble; it refuses to accept the idea "that we must do it the way it has always been done," but instead fights to guide and shape the future in the best possible way.

The Modern Olympic Movement also has been influenced by Baron de Coubertin's study of the ancient Games and their ideals, especially the sacred truce which halted all hostilities during the Games. In seeking to expand on these ideals, the IOC has worked to abolish racial discrimination, to reduce social inequalities, to unite communities, to improve the quality of life around the world, and to strengthen and consolidate world peace. "Peace," Coubertin believed, "could be the product only of a better world; a better world could be brought about only by better individuals; and better individuals could be developed only by the give and take, the buffering and battering, the stress and strain of free competition."

Olympic Symbols

Baron de Coubertin wanted to use sports to improve the health and values of youth and to celebrate the competition of talented individual athletes. In addition, he expected the Olympic Games to provide an opportunity for individuals from different countries and cultures to become friends with each other.

We can find examples of this international search for peace and goodwill in various Olympic symbols and activities.

The Olympic Torch and Flame

The torch is usually passed hand-to-hand by relays of runners starting from the original site of the Olympic Games at Olympia, Greece, to the main stadium of the current Games. As a symbol of peace among peoples, the flame represents the basic spiritual significance of the Ancient and Modern Olympic Movement.

The Olympic Rings

The five interlocking rings (reproduced here in black and white) represent the five areas of the world that accept the Olympic ideals. In every flag of the world there can be found at least one color of the colored rings. The colors from left to right are blue, yellow, black, green, and red on a white background.

The Doves of Peace

A symbol of peace, the doves are released at each of the opening ceremonies to remind people everywhere that as in ancient times the Olympic Games should be held in an atmosphere of peace.

The Olympic Motto

Finally, the goals of the Olympic Movement are summarized in the Olympic Motto. "Citius, Altius, Fortius" expresses the aspirations of the Olympic Movement. Loosely translated, these Latin words mean "Swifter, Higher, Stronger."

Olympism in Today's World

The term "Olympism" is new to most Americans, although it has been widely used in other countries for some years. It is not an easy term to grasp. Indeed, rarely do two people define it the same way, even though most definitions emphasize the positive and constructive value of the Olympic spirit and ideals.

> Olympism is a state of mind, a philosophy even, encompassing a particular concept of modern sport, according to which sport can, through an extension of its practice, play a part in the development of the individual, and of humankind in general ... and to strengthen understanding and friendship among peoples.
>
> The IOC, 1989

Let's not be overly complicated: Olympism is essentially the foundation upon which the entire Olympic Movement rests. Below are a few major points that expand on the themes relating to Olympism, introduced in Chapter 1, with which most everyone agrees:

(1) It stresses the development of physical skills, aims at improving the mind, and seeks to create a well-rounded individual. To this end, it teaches self-confidence, respect for others, faith in ideals, independence of mind and action, and a sense of social obligation.

(2) It recognizes honest and fair competition on equal terms and sets a specific and tangible example to the people who compete with one another in other fields of social activity.

(3) It recognizes and extols individual effort and accepts no discrimination among nations, races, political systems, classes, etc. It embraces world society, and cultivates the spirit of mutual cooperation and friendship among all people.

(4) It involves not only those individuals involved in competitive sport, but the general public, as it is available to all ages, all levels of athletic skills, all social strata, and all men and women through the Olympic Movement.

Being involved in training and competition should be regarded as preparation for a future career in life, *not a goal in itself.*

The Athlete's Creed

"The most important thing in the Olympic Games is not to win but to take part, just as the most important thing in life is not the triumph but the struggle. The essential thing is not to have conquered but to have fought well."

The International Olympic Academy

Once again it was Baron de Coubertin who provided the initial idea of a cultural institution that could provide the Olympic Movement with an educational philosophy which would link body and mind.

In 1961, the International Olympic Academy was established next to the ancient Olympic Stadium in Olympia, Greece. The Academy was a gift of the Greek Olympic Committee to the Olympic Movement. It functions under the auspices of the IOC through a special commission.

Students, educators, and scientists from different areas of study have visited the Academy every summer but one, when civil strife interfered, since 1961. There they participate in conferences and seminars which examine various problems confronting Olympism, delve into the philosophy and history of the Olympic Games, and examine new ways to spread the Olympic principles to schools and universities, as well as to the general public. Also, over sixty countries throughout the world now hold their own National Olympic Academy meetings.

In this fashion, the Academy has taken on an important role in the Olympic Movement.

Is Winning Everything?

Of course everyone wants to win. All people want to be liked, admired, and respected for their achievements. It is perfectly normal to want to win, and winning is a worthwhile goal.

Where all of this can go terribly wrong is when winning becomes the all-consuming goal. That is, when the desire to win is so great that it causes one to consider dishonest and excessive methods.

At the ancient Greek games, athletes caught cheating were forced to pay for statues of Zeus. These were lined up at the entrance to the stadium, and all competitors had to pass by them as they entered the stadium.

One such method of cheating today is the use of illegal (and usually harmful) drugs, seeking to enhance athletic performance. Increasingly, athletic organizations are insisting that competitors subject themselves to drug tests, and they are punishing those individuals found to have taken drugs.

In 1988, Ben Johnson of Canada broke the world record in the 100-meter dash, but lost the record and the gold medal when he was disqualified because anabolic steroids showed up in his urine sample.

Failure to abide by the rules *and* the spirit of the rules is destructive to the sport. When players use illegal tactics—such as holding, pushing, tripping, etc.—even without being detected, they have violated *the letter of the rules*. When such illegal tactics are taught to players, the coaches have violated *the spirit of the rules* and, indeed, *the spirit* of all competitive athletics.

Olympic Oath

"In the name of all competitors, I promise that we shall take part in these Olympic Games, respecting and abiding by the rules which govern them, committing ourselves to a sport without doping and without drugs, in the true spirit of sportsmanship, for the glory of sport and the honor of our teams."

When athletes lose their self-control and attack their opponents or heatedly protest the decisions of referees or judges, they have usually violated *the letter of the rules* and, most certainly, *the spirit of the rules*. When coaches, school officials, parents, or spectators lose their self-control, they set a most unfortunate example, and dishonor the sport.

Fair competition, the Olympic ideal, is based upon two basic premises:

- that athletes abide by the rules and not seek unfair advantage; and

- that athletes treat each other not as enemies but as co-players who, while competing fiercely against each other, afford each other the respect due to comrades in the same sport.

Think About It—

Opponents are necessary partners—how can we have sports events without them?

It is impossible to have a competitive sporting event without rules or referees to ensure that they are followed. When the rules are consistently broken and the judges ignored, that sport disintegrates and is in danger of becoming a farce.

A Triumph of Sportsmanship

Many people today believe that the 1936 Olympic Games in Berlin were marred because the spirit of good competition was invaded by Adolf Hitler's politics. But, in the hearts of some athletes, the Olympic spirit was very strong. Luz Long, a German long jumper, was the perfect model for Hitler to prove his theory that the Nazis' Aryan race was superior. Jesse Owens, an African-American athlete who had already won the gold medal in the 100-meter dash, was the one man capable of ruining Hitler's show.

Owens, however, had trouble landing on the 23 foot 5-1/2 inch mark to qualify for the long jump finals. When Owens took what he thought was a practice run into the pit, it was counted as his first jump by officials. Slightly shaken, he then fouled on his second try. As the American prepared for his final attempt, Long tapped Owens on the shoulder and advised Owens that if he moved his mark back one foot and didn't try to hit the take-off board, he would qualify for the finals.

Not only did Owens qualify [following this advice], he won the finals, leaping to an Olympic record of 26 feet 5-1/2 inches. Long received the silver medal and then congratulated the man that Hitler had called "inferior."

Atlanta Committee for the Olympic Games,
Olympic Handout #15

Jesse Owens

Leading Olympic Medal Winners, 2000 Olympic Games

Country	Gold	Silver	Bronze	Total
United States	39	25	33	97
Russia	32	28	28	88
China	28	16	15	59
Australia	16	25	17	58
Germany	14	17	26	57
France	13	14	11	38
Italy	13	8	13	34
Cuba	11	11	7	29
Great Britain	11	10	7	28
South Korea	8	9	11	28
Romania	11	6	9	26
Netherlands	12	9	4	25
Ukraine	3	10	10	23
Japan	5	8	5	18
Hungary	8	6	3	17
Belarus	3	3	11	17
Poland	6	5	3	14
Canada	3	3	8	14
Bulgaria	5	6	2	13
Greece	4	6	3	13
Sweden	4	5	3	12
Brazil	0	6	6	12
Spain	3	3	5	11
Norway	4	3	3	10
Switzerland	1	6	2	9
Ethiopia	4	1	3	8
Czech Republic	2	3	3	8
Kazakhstan	3	4	0	7
Kenya	2	3	2	7
Jamaica	0	4	3	7
Denmark	2	3	1	6
Indonesia	1	3	2	6
Mexico	1	2	3	6
Georgia	0	0	6	6

4

Olympic Sports

The various international sports federations choose the disciplines, events, and sports for each of the Olympic Games. To qualify as an Olympic sport, that sport must be widely practiced by men in at least 75 countries and on four continents, and by women in at least 40 countries and on three continents. Sports widely practiced in at least 25 countries and on three continents may be included in the Winter Games.

In the past, the host country occasionally has been allowed to include one or two demonstration sports. If there is enough interest, they may be selected as medal sports in future Games. For example, tennis and baseball were demonstration sports before becoming medal sports in the 1988 and 1992 Games, respectively.

Lillehammer Winter Games—1994
61 events: 34 (men), 25 (women), and 2 (mixed).

Atlanta Summer Games—1996
275 events: 165 (men), 99 (women), and 11 (mixed).

Nagano Winter Games—1998
68 events: 37 (men), 29 (women), and 2 (mixed).

Sydney Summer Games—2000
300 events: 168 (men), 120 (women), and 12 (mixed).

©1988 USOC

ARCHERY

Some authorities date the origin of archery as far back as 25,000 B.C. The earliest people known to have used the bow and arrow were the ancient Egyptians, who adopted the weapon at least 5,000 years ago. The basics of archery are still the same; however, the modern bows used in the sport are not. They are incredibly complicated, augmented by bowsights, bowmarks, foresights, and stabilizers.

Olympic archers must have exceptional control, concentration, and upper-body strength to give the arrows the speed and accuracy needed to hit their target. The standard target is 1.22 meters, and there is a standard distance of 70 meters for all events.

Scoring

The circular target has a series of concentric rings around a solid gold center, or "bull's-eye." Ranging outward from the bull's-eye, the colors of the rings are red, blue, black, and white. The rings are assigned point values for arrows shot into them ranging from 10 for a bull's-eye to 1 point for an arrow in the outer white ring.

> *Striking the target dead-center is somewhat like standing on the goal line of a football field and hitting an apple under the opposite goal post.*

Competition

Men and women compete in separate divisions, and the top 64 men and 64 women from the qualifying rounds then enter head-to-head direct elimination matches. The winner of each match advances until the gold medal winner is determined. Matches use 18 arrows until the quarterfinals, semifinals, and finals, which are 12-arrow matches.

> *Archers can propel arrows at speeds of more than 150 miles per hour.*

©1988 USOC

ATHLETICS:
TRACK AND FIELD

The basics of athletics—running, jumping, and throwing—are also the basics of every sport ever devised. Men and women in prehistoric times jumped because there were no bridges and ran to escape wild beasts. Sometimes they had to run after the beasts for food, and once drawing close enough, they would throw something, at first a stone, and then later a primitive wooden spear.

By the time of the ancient Olympic Games in Greece, running, jumping, and throwing had become very competitive. Contestants from all over Greece made the trek to Olympia to display their athletic prowess.

Running

Starting positions of the 200- and 400-meter dashes and the 4 x 100-meter relay are staggered to prevent runners in the outer lanes from having to cover a greater distance.

Dashes

The very first race of the modern Olympics was the opening heat of the 100-meter dash. Also known as sprints, dashes are the shortest and swiftest running events. Distances are 100, 200, and 400 meters. A fast start is especially important in sprinting. The athlete crouches at the starting line, leaps into full stride at the crack of the starter's pistol, and races to the finish line at top speed. Sprinters usually attain speeds of roughly 27 miles per hour. Efficient sprinting is achieved by lifting the knees high, allowing free-swinging arm movements, and leaning forward about 25 degrees.

Middle-Distance Runs

Races ranging from 800 meters to 1,500 meters are often referred to as middle-distance events. The standard Olympic middle-distance events are the 800- and 1,500- meter races for women and men. (The 3,000-meter race for women has been discontinued, and the men's 3,000 is a steeplechase.)

Distance Runs

The 10,000 meter is the longest race run on a track in the Olympic Games. To prevent exhaustion, any excess motion is avoided. The knee action is slight, arm movements are reduced to a minimum, and the strides are kept short.

The most grueling distance run is the marathon. It is the ultimate test of endurance. Good marathoners learn how to maintain their rhythm, how to keep from trailing by too much or making their move too soon, and how to preserve their energy for the final stretch.

Relays

Relay races are events for teams of four individuals in which each athlete runs a prescribed distance, called a leg, then passes a hollow tube (called a "baton") to a succeeding team member. In the 4 x 100-meter relay each team member runs 100 meters, and in the 4 x 400-meter relay each member runs 400 meters.

Hurdling

Hurdling events are dashes in which competitors must clear a series of ten barriers called "hurdles." Hurdlers need to lean forward and clear each barrier smoothly without breaking the rhythm of the running stride. The first leg to clear the hurdle is brought quickly down to the track, while the trailing leg clears the hurdle at almost a right angle to the body. Running speed, flexibility, and superior coordination are important elements of success.

Racewalk

In the sport of racewalking, women compete in a 20-kilometer event, while men compete in the 20- and 50-kilometer events. Walking is defined as a succession of steps, during which there must be contact with the ground at all times. The heel of the forward foot must touch the track before the toe of the trailing foot leaves the ground. If a competitor's walking action breaks contact with the ground, the walker may be cautioned or even disqualified for succeeding infractions.

Steeplechase

The steeplechase is an obstacle race run over a 3,000-meter course. It contains hurdles and one water jump and replaced the men's 3,000-meter middle-distance run at Sydney.

Jumps

The competitor has the option of jumping or "passing" during the high jump and pole vault competitions. Credit is given only for the height that has actually been cleared. With three missed attempts in a row at a selected height, the athlete is eliminated.

High Jump

The aim in high jumping is to leap over a bar resting between two upright standards. The contestant is allowed three attempts to clear each height. The "Fosbury Flop" is the most common style used today to clear the bar. This maneuver was named for its originator, the American Dick Fosbury, who used it to win this event in the 1968 Olympics. To execute the flop, jumpers twist on takeoff in front of the crossbar, rise above the bar headfirst, clear the bar with their backs facing the ground, and land on the foam pad with their shoulders.

Pole Vault

In pole vaulting, the athlete attempts to clear a crossbar with the aid of a long flexible pole. Grasping the pole near its top, the vaulter races down a runway, digs the tip of the pole into a box or slot in the ground, and swings upward toward the bar. The vaulter then drops onto a foam padding, called the pit.

Long Jump

Long jumping requires strong leg and abdominal muscles, running speed, and superior jumping ability. The athlete dashes down a runway, hits a takeoff board, and springs forward, attempting to cover the greatest possible distance.

Triple Jump

The aim in the triple jump is to leap the greatest distance possible in a series of three quick steps. In the first phase the jumper sprints along a running path, and "hops" into the air from a

Ray Ewry of the United States won eight gold medals in
jumping events in the 1900, 1904, and 1908 Olympic Games.

takeoff board. The jumper then springs or "steps" forward and
then "jumps" into the air once more and lands on both feet, in a
manner similar to the long jumper.

Throws

For a throw to be counted as fair and measured for distance, the
object must land within a designated area, and the athlete must
have thrown it while remaining within the throwing circle or
behind the scratch line.

Shot Put

The object of shotputting is to propel a solid metal ball through
the air as far as possible. The athlete holds the shot in the fingers
of the throwing hand and rests the hand against the shoulder,

under the chin. The competitor then bounds across the 2.135-meter circle in a half crouch, building up speed. Upon reaching the opposite side of the circle, the competitor puts the shot with an explosive uncoiling of the arm and body. The shot is pushed into the air, not thrown. The men's shot weighs 7.26 kilograms; the women's shot weighs 4 kilograms.

Discus Throw

The discus throw is one of the oldest of all Olympic events, clearly tracing its origins to the early Greeks. The discus thrower is the image most often depicted in Greek art.

The discus is a steel-rimmed hardwood or metal platter that is thrown from a circle 2.5 meters in diameter. The athlete holds the discus flat against the palm and forearm, then whirls around, rapidly propelling the discus outward with a whipping motion of the arm. The men's discus weighs about 2 kilograms; the women's weighs about 1 kilogram.

Hammer Throw

Hammer throwers compete by hurling a ball attached to a length of wire that has a metal handle. Gripping the handle with both hands and keeping the feet in place, the athlete whirls the ball around in a circle passing above and behind the head and just below the kneecaps. As the hammer gains momentum, the athlete suddenly whirls the body around three times. The hammer is then released upward and outward at a 45-degree angle and must fall within a 45-degree sector. The hammer weighs 7.26 kilograms for men and 4 kilograms for women; the length for both is approximately 1.2 meters.

Javelin Throw

Contestants grasp the javelin, which is a steel-tipped metal spear, near its center of gravity and sprint toward a check line. Drawing back the javelin, they execute a hop or fast cross step. At the scratch line, they pivot forward abruptly and hurl the javelin into the air. The throw is "fouled" if they step across the line or if the javelin does not fall to earth point first, or does not land within the prescribed sector.

Mildred "Babe" Didrikson threw the javelin a world-record distance in the 1932 Olympic Games.

The men's javelin weighs 80 grams and measures a minimum of 2.6 meters in length. The women's javelin weighs 600 grams and is at least 2.2 meters in length.

Decathlon

The men's decathlon is a two-day, ten-event contest that places a premium on athleticism, stamina, and versatility. The events included are the 100-meter dash, long jump, shot put, high jump, 400-meter run, 110-meter high hurdles, discus throw, pole vault, javelin throw, and 1,500-meter run. The athlete's performance in the various events is rated against a complex scoring table. The highest point total determines the winner.

Heptathlon

The women's pentathlon began in the 1920s and was added to the Olympic Summer Games in 1964. Twenty years later, the heptathlon was introduced to the Olympic program at the Olympic Summer Games in Los Angeles, replacing the five-event pentathlon. This new combined event for women added two events—the javelin throw and an 800-meter run—to the five in the original pentathlon, which were the 100-meter high hurdles, shot put, high jump, long jump, and 200-meter run.

©1988 USOC

BADMINTON

Olympic badminton is considerably different from the backyard game that Americans play for recreation. It's the world's second-fastest racket sport (with jai alai coming in first). Instead of a ball, the game is played with a shuttlecock, a cork ball fitted with stabilizing feathers, which is also known as a "cock" or "bird." This bird can be propelled over the net at speeds of up to 200 miles per hour.

Badminton debuted as a full-medal sport at the 1992 Games in Barcelona, Spain.

Badminton is a game that somewhat resembles tennis. It can be played by two or four players, either indoors or outdoors. A net is stretched across the middle of the court with the top edge 1.524 meters from the ground at the center and 1.55 meters at the posts. The players hit the shuttlecock back and forth over the net with lightweight rackets.

Competition

For each game, badminton scoring begins at 0-0 (called "love-all") and 15 points wins a game. One point is scored if the serving side wins a rally. They then get to serve from the alternate service court. If the receiving side wins the rally, the score does not change. The service goes to the next player in turn.

In singles, the service goes to the opponent. In doubles, it is the partner who gets the next serve. However, if both doubles partners have just taken turns serving, then the service goes to one of their opponents.

If the score is 14-14, the side that reached 14 points first can choose to play to 15 points, or they can "set" the game to 17 points. The final score is the sum of the points won before "setting," plus the points won during "setting."

In women's singles, 11 points wins a game. If the score reaches 10-10, the game can be "set" to 13 points.

There are competitions for both singles and doubles in which men and women compete separately. However, starting at Atlanta in 1996, mixed doubles were played. All matches are played the best two out of three games.

©1988 USOC

BASEBALL

Often referred to as America's "national pastime," baseball made its debut as an official Olympic sport on July 26, 1992, in Barcelona, Spain. Baseball, however, often had been seen in various exhibition and demonstration games throughout modern Olympic history.

Originally introduced to the Olympics in 1912, the teams were made up of players who were already competing in other official events. In 1936 two American teams of amateurs played as an exhibition game, and it was so popular that it was scheduled to become an official sport at the 1940 Olympic Games in Japan. However, due to World War II, the Games were canceled and baseball would be overlooked as an official Olympic sport for the next 52 years.

Baseball reappeared unofficially in 1952. Initially, it was restricted to a single game format (win and advance, lose and be eliminated). Olympic baseball began following a tournament format at the 1984 Games in Los Angeles. Shortly after this, the

International Olympic Committee formally decided baseball would be an official sport in 1992.

Scoring

Each game is to be nine innings long with three outs per side in each inning. Three strikes equal an out. Four balls out of the strike zone not swung at by the batter result in a "walk." A run scores when a batter safely reaches all four bases—first, second, and third bases, and home plate.

One notable change to the traditional baseball rules is that the game ends if the "home" team leads by 10 or more runs after 6 1/2 innings or if the "visitors" lead by that same margin after 7 innings.

Competition

In what might be referred to quite literally as a "World Series," qualifying baseball teams from around the globe battle each other in a round-robin-style competition with the top four teams advancing to the semifinals. The two winning teams then advance to the finals to compete for the gold and silver medals while the other two teams play for the bronze.

©1988 USOC

BASKETBALL

Men's Olympic basketball became an official sport in 1936 at the Berlin Games. The tournament was held outdoors in a tennis stadium on courts of clay and sand. During the tournament, a rule was passed that banned all players who were taller than 6 feet 3 inches. The United States, which would have lost three of its players, objected, and the rule was withdrawn. On the day of the final it rained heavily, turning the courts to mud. It was very difficult to dribble on wet sand, which undoubtedly contributed to the low score of 19-8 with the United States defeating Canada for the gold.

The United States continued to win gold medals at the next six consecutive Olympic Games, entering the finals in 1972 with a record of 62 wins and no losses in Olympic play. The winning streak ended at that game with a 50-51 loss to the U.S.S.R. There was so much controversy surrounding that game that the members of the U.S. team voted unanimously to refuse their silver medals in protest.

In 1989 the Federation Internationale de Basketball Amateur (FIBA) membership overwhelmingly voted to allow professionals to join amateurs in the Olympics. The United States then assembled an all-star National Basketball Association (NBA) "Dream Team" for the 1992 Games, which easily walked away with the gold.

Women's basketball made its Olympic debut at the 1976 Games in Montreal, Canada. The Soviet women were undefeated coming into the Olympics, and predictably won the gold medal. The U.S. women's team, however, did extremely well in this inaugural event, taking home a well-deserved silver medal.

Scoring

The rules are the same for both men and women in Olympic play. Foul shots count for 1 point and ordinary field goals (or baskets)2 points. A field goal is worth 3 points if it is shot from outside the 3-point field goal line.

The offensive team has 30 seconds in which to shoot on a court that is 28 meters long and 15 meters wide. This is slightly smaller than the court used by American collegians and professionals. Play consists of two 20-minute halves, separated by a 10-minute halftime break.

While the "alley oop" shot (a pass received near the basket rim by a leaping player who jams the ball in the basket while still in the air) is legal in the United States, it is not allowed in Olympic play. However, touching the ball while it's on the rim ("goaltending") is allowed in Olympic Games but not in the NBA.

©1988 USOC

BIATHLON

Biathlon, from the Greek word meaning "two tests," is a combination of cross-country skiing and rifle shooting. Competitions were recorded as early as 1767 between "ski-runner companies," which guarded the Swedish-Norwegian border. Later competitions were held to promote national defense at the local level. In France, the biathlon (known as the military patrol) made its demonstration debut in the first Olympic Winter Games in 1924. It was eliminated after the 1948 Olympics due to the antimilitary atmosphere surrounding the Games. The biathlon was re-introduced to the Olympic Winter Games as an official sport in 1960.

Competition

The biathlon requires a combination of incredible stamina, cross-country skiing, and precision rifle shooting. The skiing segment of the biathlon is a physically demanding strength event, while the shooting segment is a technique event that calls for keen concentration and a steady hand. During the event, the athletes ski cross-country along a winding course with rifles slung across their backs. At set points along the track, they must stop and fire at fixed targets as steadily and accurately as they can. Competitors usually slow down slightly as they approach the range area in an attempt to control their breathing and slow down their racing heartbeats.

An athlete takes 25 seconds to a minute at each firing range. At these stops, the competitor unslings the rifle, flips off the snow cover that protects the sight, assumes the appropriate prone or standing shooting position, inserts a magazine—a device for holding shells, also called *cartridges*—into the rifle, aims, fires, flips the sight cover back on, slings the rifle, and continues on the course. Remember, the athlete actually manages to do all this in only 25 seconds to one minute.

In individual competitions, a one-minute penalty is added to the skiing time for each target missed. In the sprint events, the competitor skis one penalty loop for each target missed. If, after eight shots during the relay competitions, targets remain unhit, the athlete must ski a corresponding number of penalty loops. The time it takes to ski around the penalty loop is then added to the final skiing time.

©1988 USOC

BOBSLED

The first organized bobsled competition was held in Saint Moritz, Switzerland, in 1898. Bobsled teams competed in the first Winter Olympics in 1924, and the event was included regularly in the Games thereafter. In these early days of sledding, a temporary barrier was set up in front of the sled before the start of the race. When this barrier was removed, the team members would bob their heads and upper bodies in unison. This action, which gives bobsledding its name, starts the sled and propels it down the course.

The Sled

A typical bobsled consists of two small sleds connected by a semi-flexible steel platform. The crew sits on the platform. Team members steer by means of a rope or wheel attached to the front sled. Racing sleds have been clocked at speeds up to 118 miles per hour; however, they generally average between 60 and 70 miles per hour. Given the minimal chassis of the sleds and the high speeds, competitors experience bone-crunching jolts over even the smallest of bumps. Small errors in course setting and delayed reactions can send the sleds and their passengers bouncing sideways down chutes.

Although racing bobsleds are equipped with brakes, the brakeman is not allowed to use them, except to slow down the sled after it crosses the finish line.

The most critical part of a bobsled run is its start. Team members sprint while pushing the sled forward in order to gain momentum. Before the first turn, the sledders leap into their positions on the sled in rapid succession, and assume streamlined positions for the remainder of the run.

The Rules

Most of the rules of bobsledding involve the design and construction of the racing sleds. These rules are extremely detailed and designed to equalize the equipment used by the different teams.

The basic rules are the same for both the two-man and the four-man teams. Each team is allowed to make four runs (or heats), on two successive days, down the chute. The same people must be on the sled for each run. The times of all four runs are added together, and the lowest combined time wins the event. Start order is determined by drawing lots for the first heat, then alternating the start order for each subsequent heat to equalize the ice conditions in the chute.

©1988 USOC

BOXING

Quite a few Olympic boxers have gone on to become world champions—gold medalists Sugar Ray Leonard (1976), Leon Spinks (1976), Michael Spinks (1976), George Foreman (1968), Joe Frazier (1964), Muhammad Ali [Cassius Clay] (1960), and Floyd Patterson (1952)—just to name a few. Olympic boxers must be between the ages of 17 and 32; competitions are held in 12 weight divisions ranging from light flyweight (up to 48 kg, or about 106 lb) to super heavyweight (over 91 kg, or more than 200 lb).

Scoring

Olympic-style boxing is faster than the professional game, and the rules are vastly different as well. The scoring system in amateur boxing awards a point to the fighter who can connect with a punch and move away before his opponent can do the same. All legal blows are scored equally. Pushing an opponent or pinning him against the ropes with the shoulder or forearm are both allowed in professional boxing, but in Olympic boxing they are punished.

Infractions may result in point deductions and, in extreme cases, disqualification. Punches that count have to be delivered by the white part of the glove covering the knuckles. To be scored, a blow must be clean, fair, and judged substantial.

Competition

Olympic boxing matches, or bouts, consist of four 2-minute rounds. Five judges sitting ringside score the bout using a computer with a program that electronically tabulates each boxer's scoring punches. A judge must press either a red or a blue button on his keyboard when the "red" or "blue" fighter throws what the judge considers to be a scoring punch. Three of five judges must press either the red or blue button within one second (starting when any one judge presses his button) for a point to register for a boxer.

Tie scores are rare, but they do occur; in such cases, the highest and lowest scores are dropped. In the unlikely event the score is still tied, each of the five judges votes for a winner by pressing the red or blue button on his keyboard. The boxer chosen by at least three of the five judges wins.

Winning by points is the most common way to win a match, but not the only way. A boxer can forfeit the match by "throwing in the towel" or can be prohibited from continuing if the referee considers him outclassed or not "giving 100 percent."

A match is stopped if one of the boxers is knocked down and receives an eight-count three times in one round or four times in a bout. A boxer is considered "down" if he touches the floor with anything other than his feet, or if he is even partially outside the ropes as a result of a punch. If a boxer remains "down" to a full count of ten, the bout ends by a knockout.

©1988 USOC

CANOE/KAYAK

Canoes and kayaks bring to mind serene images of gliding down a calm river or across a cool lake. However, canoe/kayak contests can be fiercely competitive. There are different events for each craft, but both feature races that are breathtakingly close. Competitors speed past the finish line only fractions of a second apart.

For both canoes and kayaks, there are two types of competitions in two separate environments: sprints in (calm) flatwater, and slaloms in (more turbulent) whitewater. Flatwater sprint canoe/kayak racing has been an Olympic event since 1936, but whitewater slalom racing got a late start. Appearing for the first time in 1972, it was not seen again until the 1992 Games in Barcelona.

There are more differences between the sports of canoeing and kayaking than one might imagine. A kayak is closed, except for the small cockpit where the paddler sits; a flatwater canoe is open, and in whitewater it is equipped with a watertight sprayskirt. A kayaker uses a double-bladed paddle while a canoeist uses one with a single blade, paddling alternately from side to side. A canoeist kneels while paddling; a kayaker sits in the boat with legs extended forward.

Even though the kayak and canoe are generally similar in shape, the canoe is slightly larger and weighs considerably more.

Whitewater Slalom

Whitewater slalom requires the paddler to navigate an obstacle course in much the same manner as the slalom races in skiing. Each competitor runs the course twice, counting only the better score. Time penalties are assessed for improper negotiation of gates (touching a gate, intentionally moving the poles, or missing the gate altogether).

Competition

The contests begin with qualifying heats. The first three finishers in each heat advance directly to the semifinals. The others take part in a *repechage*, or second-chance round (*repechage* being the French word for "fishing again"), for another chance to advance to the semifinals. The paddlers with the top three times in each of three semifinals compete in the finals.

©1998 USOC

CURLING

Although curling has been played for almost five centuries, its origins are obscure. The name "curling" is derived from the action which causes a polished stone to turn as it is released and curl to the right or left as it slides along the ice. Some believe that it started in the Low Countries of Europe, while others argue that it was invented by Scots looking for a way to pass the time after the lochs froze over. Scotland's claims are bolstered by the fact that it has the first written references to curling dating back to 1638. Regardless of where the game originated, the Scots nurtured and exported the sport to the rest of the world.

While the Scots may have invented the game, it was the Canadians who developed it. At the present time, curling rivals hockey as Canada's national game, and the Canadians have dominated the annual World Curling Championship. Curling made its debut as an Olympic medal sport at Nagano, Japan, in 1998.

The game consists of two teams of four players. One player curls the stone, while two others run ahead and sweep the surface of the ice with brooms to speed up or redirect the shot. Ten "ends" or periods consisting of two curls per player make up a game.

The rink is approximately 146 feet long and 15 feet 7 1/2 inches wide, with two 12-foot (3.7 m) houses on each end. The bull's-eye is located in the middle of the house and is 4 feet (1.2 m) in diameter. Players wear special ice shoes with a nonstick-coated "slider" on one foot and a crepe sole on the other foot. The stones resemble teakettles minus the spout, with a handle on one end. They are polished granite rocks, 21 inches (53 cm) in diameter. They weigh 42 pounds (19 kg) each. There are two types of long-handled brooms or brushes: a corn-bloom broom and a bristle broom.

Curling involves a strategy like chess. Watch the different shots that are being called and then attempted. The ability of the player to make shots and the teamwork involving curling and sweeping are the integral aspects of the sport.

Scoring

Similar to shuffleboard, players compete by alternating turns curling heavy stones across a large level sheet of ice, attempting to stop the stones closest to a target dyed into the ice, called a house. Points are scored by the team with the stones closest to the house. The strategy involves knocking the opponents' stones off the target or blocking the opponent from getting at one's own stone that is in good position.

CYCLING

Olympic cycling includes both individual and team competitions over different types of terrain, and each race varies in distance from just a single kilometer to more than 200. In some events, it's cyclist versus cyclist; in others, the race is just against the clock.

Traditionally, Olympic cycling had two distinct categories of racing: road and track. Track events occur on steeply-banked tracks called *velodromes*. Road racing is exactly what the name implies—racing on paved roadways. In 1996, mountain bike racing made its debut at Atlanta, bringing a third dimension to cycling: off-road racing. The only mountain bike event at Sydney was a cross-country (XC) competition held on a circuit made up of off-road trails, unpaved roads (dirt or gravel), and forest roads.

The Races

In the time trials, competitors race against the clock to record the fastest time. Time trials are considered to be the ultimate challenge in cycling, as this is an all-out race for the fastest time and requires a great deal of strength. A cyclist is said to have "hit the wall" when his legs can no longer pedal at a rapid pace.

Match sprints are three laps, with riders seeded on the basis of a 200-meter time trial. In the time trials, each cyclist is given a lap to gain momentum and then is timed for the last 200 meters.

In pursuit races, two cyclists or teams of cyclists start off on opposite sides of the track. If one cyclist, or team, catches the other, the race is over. Otherwise, the winner is the first one to cross the finish line.

Points races can be the most fun to watch but are among the most difficult to understand. Varying points are awarded to the first four cyclists during lap sprints, which occur every fifth lap. Double points are awarded to the four leading cyclists at the halfway point and last lap. The cyclist who has the most points usually wins; however, a rider can also win if he laps the field (goes ahead of everyone else by a lap) and maintains his advantage throughout the race regardless of his total points.

Road races are mass-start events that take place on public roads. Endurance is the main factor in road racing, as it takes several hours to finish these races. Riding in the slipstream (current of air created by the leader) decreases wind resistance and can cut a cyclist's effort by as much as 20 percent. This is also called "drafting" and can be utilized in all cycling events.

Other mountain bike events include the dual slalom (DS), where two riders race head-to-head down parallel slalom courses. Observed trials (OT) are rides over an obstacle course which usually includes mud, rocks, water, or any other natural obstacles. Short track cross-country is a new mountain biking event that is a short-loop circuit race about 1.21km (.75 mi) in distance and is ridden around the central area of the track.

©1988 USOC

DIVING

Since divers and swimmers both end up in water, they're mistakenly linked in the minds of most viewers. However, diving actually has more in common with gymnastics than it does with swimming. Fancy diving is believed to have begun in the 1800s as part of the gymnastics movement that was popular throughout Germany and Sweden. These gymnasts performed their acrobatics over lakes and rivers throughout Northern Europe.

Technique

Fancy dives are classified into four basic types: (1) the layout, (2) the pike, (3) the tuck, and (4) the freestyle. In the layout or "straight" dive, the body must not be bent in any fashion. The arms are kept straight and the feet together. In the pike, the body is bent at the hips and the knees are kept rigid. In the tuck, the body is compactly bunched with thighs drawn to the chest. The fourth dive, the freestyle, is not an actual body position, but signifies a diver's option to use any of the other three positions or combinations of them to complete a single dive. The freestyle may include twists or other intricate movements in the air.

The diver's entry into the water should be as vertical as possible and completed with little or no splash.

In the attempt to execute a dive with no splash, divers use a form that is referred to as a "rip" entry. As the diver readies himself for the dive, he grabs the top of the knuckle and finger area of one hand, extends the arms, and pulls the hands back, so that the palm of the bottom hand hits the water first. When done correctly, this entry enables the diver to enter the water with the smallest amount of splash possible and produces a sound like a bag ripping.

Competition

Both men and women compete separately in three events: the 3-meter springboard, the 10-meter platform, and synchronized diving.

Springboard diving is performed from a springboard 3 meters above the water. Since 1964, Olympic competitions have begun with a preliminary round of 7 dives. The top 12 divers then advance to the finals, which consist of 11 dives—5 required and 6 voluntary. The judges' scores are multiplied by a coefficient that is determined by the degree of difficulty of the attempted dive.

Platform diving is staged from a rigid platform 10 meters above the water. The finalists perform 4 compulsory dives and 6 voluntary dives.

Men's and women's synchronized diving debuted at the 2000 Olympic Summer Games at Sydney. Pairs of men and pairs of women competed for an additional 24 diving medals—the largest number ever to be awarded at the Olympics. The two diving competitions were from the 3-meter springboard, where divers dove off adjacent boards at the same time, and the 10-meter platform, where divers dove from the same platform.

©1988 USOC

EQUESTRIAN

Equestrian displays and competitions were featured in the early Olympic Games in Greece. Public displays of horses and horsemanship reached an all-time high during the Middle Ages. Large crowds attended tournaments where armored knights jousted with each other and exhibited their equestrian skills. Today, equestrian events are still popular and have been featured in the modern Olympic Games since 1912.

The Events

Show jumping is the most well-known equestrian event. Each horse and rider jumps two rounds of a series of obstacles placed at irregular distances from each other over a set course. Fault points are assessed if an obstacle is knocked down, if the horse balks at an obstacle, or if the time is exceeded.

The dressage competition requires the rider, man or woman, to guide the horse through a series of precise and intricate movements which display the degree of communication and cooperation between human and animal. Some of these movements include a stunning element called "the passage," which calls for a suspension of motion between each step of a trot, and another, "the piaffe," in which the animal trots in place. The better performances have the quality of a dance. Points are awarded for the proper execution of each movement.

The three-day event is so demanding that it remains the only equestrian event in which both individual and team medals are derived from the same performance.

The three-day event, also called "combined training," is a grueling test of endurance and style consisting of three parts: dressage, endurance, and show jumping. The dressage and jumping sections follow the same basic rules and scoring as do the regular dressage and jumping events. The endurance phase is a long-distance obstacle run broken into four parts: two "roads and tracks," one "steeplechase," and one "cross-country." Penalty points are assessed for falls and overtime, while bonus points can be accumulated by completing any of the four sections of the endurance run under the set time limit.

©1988 USOC

FENCING

The art of swordsmanship has been practiced since Biblical times and has evolved through the ages from deadly combat to an Olympic sport. Trigger-fast reflexes and a quick mind are needed to be able to strike without being struck.

Three swords are used in fencing competitions: the *foil*, which has a flexible rectangular blade and a blunt point; the *épée* (pronounced epp-ay), which has a rigid triangular blade with a point that is covered by a cone with barbed points; and the *sabre*, which has a flexible triangular blade with a blunt point. Individual and team competitions are held for each.

Scoring

All three weapons have been modified for electronic scoring. There are two light towers at opposite ends of the strip. When the point of the weapon is depressed, a light flashes on the sidelines signaling the touch. A flashing red or green light indicates a point or blade has landed in a valid target area on the fencer nearer that tower. The official, known as the director, must confirm the touch before it counts.

In a fencing bout, the objective is to touch your opponent with your sword. Each touch is worth one point, and the fencer who reaches 15 points first wins the bout. For a team bout, the goal is to score 45 points before the other team.

Competition

The fencers battle on a "strip," or *piste*, which is a mat 14 meters long and 1.5 meters wide. If the fencer crosses the rear boundary with both feet, the opponent is awarded a penalty touch. If he should step off the side of the strip, the other fencer is allowed to advance 1 meter toward the opponent's end of the strip.

To start the match, both opponents take the *en garde* (on guard) position. This stance is assumed with the rear arm crooked upward, and the sword arm partially extended toward the opponent. The basic attacking action is the lunge, executed by thrusting the sword arm at the target and kicking forward on the front leg. The attack is successful if a touch is scored on the valid target area. In foil fencing, only touches on the torso are counted. In épée, the entire body, head to foot, is a valid target. In sabre, the valid target is the part of the body above an imaginary line, called the saddle line. A movement of the blade designed to block an attack is called a parry.

At the Olympics, the individual competition is a direct elimination format. Bouts are in three sections of three-minutes each. If neither fencer reaches 15 touches (or hits) by the end of the third section, or round, the fencer with the most touches is the winner. In the case of a tie at the end of a regulation bout, there is one minute of extra fencing time added. The fencer scoring the first touch is the winner. The team competition consists of teams from up to 12 countries. Each match comprises nine bouts of four minutes (maximum) per bout; a bout ends when a fencer makes the next multiple of five touches or time expires.

©1988 USOC

FIELD HOCKEY

Field hockey is a noncontact sport played on the amateur level and was formalized in England in 1876. The game has since become popular throughout Europe and in India (where it is the national sport), Pakistan, Australia, New Zealand, North America, and parts of South America, Asia, and Africa.

The Olympic sport of field hockey is much closer to soccer than it is to ice hockey. The number of players (11 on a side), the field size or "pitch" (91.4 meters long by 55 meters wide), and the basic strategy are much the same in both games.

Scoring

A point is scored when a player hits the ball into the opponent's net from within the striking circle, a zone that stretches 14.6 meters in front of the goal.

Competition

The object is to score by hitting the ball into the opponent's goal with a stick that is curved at one end and flattened on one side (the striking side). Field hockey does not allow playing the ball with the feet, although the goalkeeper (goalie) may use any part of the body to stop the ball, and may kick it only when it is in the striking circle. Penalties for fouls committed in that area are more severe than for those committed outside it. A penalty stroke is awarded for an intentional foul by a defender within the circle, or when a defender stops a sure goal by committing a foul. When a foul is called by the umpire, a free hit is awarded that must be taken from where the foul occurred.

The ball is put in play in midfield through a procedure called a bully. One player from each team taps the ground and the opponent's stick three times before hitting the ball.

Each team is composed of 11 players, usually 5 forwards, 2 fullbacks, 3 halfbacks, and 1 goalkeeper, but the formation may be changed by the team captain. The game is divided into two halves of 35 minutes each, with a change of goals at the end of the first half.

In international (or tournament) play where a winner advances to another, higher round, games that are tied at the end of regulation play require a maximum of two 7 1/2-minute sudden-death overtime periods. In "sudden death," the first team to score wins. If, after two overtime periods, the score remains tied, then a penalty stroke competition may be used to determine the winner. In this competition, each team selects five players who take alternating penalty strokes against the opposing goalkeeper.

©1988 USOC

FIGURE SKATING

In early times, the ribs or shinbones of animals were tied to the feet, and skaters glided on these by propelling themselves with the aid of a spiked stick. Later, iron or steel blades were introduced. However, with the development of curved steel blades in the mid-nineteenth century, the art of figure skating was born. Originally, competitions consisted of rating the participants on their ability to follow prescribed outlines, or school figures. These patterns of two- or three-lobed figure eights were then precisely traced over and over again.

Competition

Competitions are divided into three categories: singles, pairs, and ice dancing. In singles and pairs, competition is made up of two separate segments: the original program (or short program) is scored first, followed by the free skating program (or long program). Ice dancing is made up of three parts: compulsory, original, and free.

Singles

The original program is made up of compulsory moves or elements including jumps and spins. The moves may be done in any sequence within the set time limit, performed to music chosen by the skater. The free skating program has no required elements and has a length limitation of 4 1/2 minutes for men, and 4 minutes for women. Here, skaters select their own music and choreograph the many difficult jumps, spins, footwork, and interpretive moves to best display their technical and artistic skill.

Pairs

Pairs skating is essentially the same as singles but is performed in unison by partners, with the addition of daring and often dangerous overhead lifts, throws, jumps, and spins. Shadow skating, in which partners perform identical maneuvers some distance apart, and mirror skating, where the pair's moves are in opposite directions and mirror each other, are challenging aspects of pairs skating.

Ice Dancing

Ice dancing is skated in pairs, only without the overhead lifts and jumps. The emphasis is on rhythm and musical interpretation. Compulsory competition requires each team to perform the same two selected dances that must be done in an exact manner and placement on the ice. In the original, skaters are given a prescribed rhythm and must create their own routine using that rhythm, such as the polka. In free dance, the skaters are allowed 4 minutes to display their skills using any style, music, and rhythm.

©1988 USOC

GYMNASTICS

To the ancient Greeks, physical fitness was paramount, and all Greek cities had a *gymnasia*, a courtyard for jumping, running, and wrestling. The Greeks tried to introduce gymnastics to the Romans, but the Romans found it immoral and banned the practice. For centuries, gymnastics was all but forgotten. In the nineteenth century, however, interest in gymnastics soared, and a men's gymnastics competition was included in the first modern Olympic Games in 1896. Over the years, gymnastics has undergone many changes. Originally, men's competition included swimming and running events, and did not acquire its present form until the 1924 Games in Paris. During the 1920s, women organized and participated in gymnastic events, and the first women's Olympic competition was held at the 1928 Games in Amsterdam. Both men's and women's gymnastics now attract international interest, and excellent gymnasts can be found on every continent.

Scoring

Performance is scored on a 10-point scale. For each routine, the gymnast begins with less than a perfect score—9.6 for women, 9.4 for men. From that base, judges deduct for flaws in execution, exceeding the time limit, or failing to perform a required movement. Judges can also award bonus points, up to 0.4 for women, up to 0.6 for men. Bonuses are given for outstanding execution of the most difficult moves.

Competition

Gymnastics competitions are divided into four parts—a qualifying competition, the team final, the all-around final, and the apparatus final. To qualify, gymnasts perform an optional exercise on each apparatus. (Compulsory exercises were eliminated after the Atlanta Games.) Each team from each country in the team finals is made up of six gymnasts. Five gymnasts perform unique, optional exercises on each apparatus; four scores count, with the lowest score in each rotation discarded. The sum of the top four scores is the team score. The thirty-six gymnasts who achieved the highest combined individual scores in the team finals then move on to the individual all-around final. However, only three gymnasts from each nation may compete in the final, regardless of where they ranked in the top thirty-six. Each gymnast performs an optional routine on each apparatus—four for women; six for men. However, the women's vault consists of two vaults with the scores averaged. The Olympic all-around champion is the competitor with the highest cumulative score. For the apparatus finals, the top eight scorers on each apparatus during the qualifying competition move on to this concluding event. There is a limit of two gymnasts from each nation per apparatus. Each gymnast completes one exercise on the apparatus for which he or she qualified. The exception is in the men's and women's vault, where two vaults are performed and the scores averaged for the final score.

The Apparatus

The Federation Internationale Gymnastique (FIG) has established a definite order in which gymnastics events must be performed. In the following order, men must perform the floor exercise, pommel horse, rings, vault, parallel bars, and horizontal bar. Women must perform the vault, uneven bars, balance beam, and floor exercise.

Men's Events

Floor Exercise—This routine is performed on a 12-meter-square mat. The men's routine lasts from 50 to 70 seconds and is always performed without music. Both the compulsory and the freestyle routines must include required tumbling and static maneuvers demonstrating balance, strength, flexibility, and acrobatics.

Pommel Horse—This routine is performed on a leather-covered apparatus, in the center of which are inserted two wooden pommels, or handles. The exercise is composed of clean leg swings, and the routine must cover the entire length of the horse. Each routine must include at least three scissors, in which the legs split and alternately straddle the horse with pendulum-like swinging motions. Only the hands may be used for support; no other part of the body is to touch the apparatus throughout the entire routine. The legs must remain straight and the toes pointed at all times.

Rings—The two rings are suspended from the ceiling and hang 2.55 meters above the floor. This event requires the most strength of all the gymnastic exercises. A routine consists of handstands, body swings, and the holding of static positions, such as the famous "iron cross." It is important that while the body is swinging, the rings remain motionless. The dismount usually includes difficult twists and/or somersaults.

Vault—Men use the same horse for vaulting that they do for their pommel horse routines. The athlete takes off from a springboard, pushes off with both hands placed on the surface of the apparatus, then completes his flight with acrobatic twists, turns, and somersaults before making a controlled landing. For men, most vaults are executed over the length of the "horse."

Parallel Bars—This routine is performed on two flexible parallel wooden rails. A routine employs a continuous series of swinging moves, static holds, and midair somersaults, capped by spectacular flying dismounts.

Horizontal Bar—This routine is performed on a single steel bar, 2.55 meters off the ground. A routine requires static handstands at the top of the bar, as well as one-handed and two-handed swings around the bar, somersaults, and vaults over the bar before it is grasped again. The dismount begins with giant swings that produce a high flying arc and allow for multiple twists and somersaults prior to the controlled landing.

Women's Events

Vault—The women's vaulting "horse" or apparatus has no pommels. Moreover, women approach perpendicular to the apparatus and vault it from the side. The gymnast runs full speed down a 1219-1829 cm (40-60 feet) runway and takes off from a 119.38 cm (3 feet, 11 inch) springboard. Women must execute any of three types of vaults: handstand, horizontal vault, or a vault with turns. On landing, only one step may be taken without incurring a penalty, and that step must be in the direction of the descent.

Uneven Bars—This routine is performed on a set of flexible wooden parallel bars, the uppermost set 2.45 meters and the lower set 1.65 meters above the floor. A good performance demands continuous swinging and vaulting over, under, and between the bars, with a formal mount and dismount part of the overall routine.

Balance Beam—The balance beam is 5 meters long, 10 cm wide, and 1.25 meters above the floor. A routine consists of tumbling moves, turns, leaps, and suspended static positions. The formal mount and dismount are among the most dramatic maneuvers of the entire routine.

Floor Exercise—This is considered the most artistic of all gymnastic disciplines, as it combines modern and classical dance steps with tumbling and acrobatics. The entire routine is performed to music of the gymnast's own choosing. Although there are required movements, no other event encourages such expression of personality and freedom of execution.

Rhythmic Gymnastics

This newest Olympic gymnastics discipline may be best described as a cross between a floor exercise and classical ballet. It approaches the area of dance and tends to favor the more mature gymnast. Rhythmic gymnastics requires smooth, graceful body movements while performing with handheld apparatus such as the hoop, ball, clubs, rope, and ribbon. Only one apparatus may be used at a time. Unlike the floor exercise, however, there are no airborne acrobatic moves; at least one part of the body must remain in contact with the 12-meter-square floor mat at all times. Everything is done to music, and gymnasts often choose classical or other soft, melodious tunes. (Floor exercise routines, by contrast, are often performed to jazz or other upbeat tempos.) Rhythmic events are judged on the same 10-point scale and evaluated according to choreographic quality and originality, harmony, precision, and execution.

Trampoline

Athletes perform two routines of ten skills each, which include double, triple, and twisting somersaults. Scoring is on the same 10-point scale as that used in gymnastics events.

Synchronized Trampoline—This event needs precision timing, as two athletes perform the same ten skills. They mirror one another.

Double Mini-Trampoline—This event combines the run of tumbling with the rebound of trampoline. The athlete runs, jumps onto a two-level trampoline, rebounds, and dismounts onto a landing mat. Some compare this event to springboard diving using a mat instead of water.

©1988 USOC

TEAM HANDBALL

The Olympic sport of team handball is not to be confused with the game played against a wall with a small rubber ball. In this game, men use a ball 58-60 cm in circumference, and women use a ball 54-56 cm in circumference. Team handball incorporates moves such as dribbling and passing. The court, which resembles a basketball court, is 40 meters long and 20 meters wide. Each team has seven players—six on the court and one goalie. The object of the game is to score the highest number of points by throwing the ball into the opponent's goal, which is 2 meters high and 3 meters wide.

Competition

The game is played in 30-minute halves. The rapid, continuous play is marked by spectacular leaps and dives. Players may take three steps before and after a dribble. If not moving, the player may only hold the ball for three seconds; the player must then either move, score, or pass the ball to another team member. Meanwhile, the other team is trying to gain possession of the ball by either snatching it away or intercepting a pass. The goalie may use any part of the body to defend the goal.

Both men and women compete separately during tournament-style competition. After several days of preliminary rounds, finalists advance to the gold-medal game.

©1988 USOC

ICE HOCKEY

Ice hockey, an extremely rough, action-packed game, is considered one of the fastest of all sports. It is probably a descendant of *bandy*, a sport that developed in England in the late eighteenth century. Modern ice hockey was devised in the mid-1800s by British soldiers stationed in Canada. Rules were set by students at McGill University in Montréal, Québec, in 1879. Today, ice hockey is played in over 30 countries and is the national sport of Canada. All-male and all-female teams compete in separate Olympic events.

Scoring

The object is to score points by knocking the puck into the opponent's goal. The team that scores the most goals wins the game.

> *A player who scores three goals in one game is said to have scored a "hat trick."*

Competition

Teams from the competing countries are divided into two pools. These play a round-robin in the preliminaries. The winning team of each game receives 2 points in the overall standing. The losing team receives no points and, if there is a tie or draw, each team receives 1 point.

After the preliminary round, the top three teams in the overall standings in each pool advance to the medal round, which is played in the same fashion. The country finishing with the best team record wins the gold medal.

The Game

The game is divided into three 20-minute periods. Each team has no more than six players on the ice at a time, including one goaltender, or goalie. Players wear protective pads under their clothing and thick gloves on their hands. Play begins with a face-off, when the referee drops the puck between the opposing centers. Teams attempt to score by passing and shooting the puck across the ice with their sticks.

Penalties are assessed for holding, tripping, slashing with the stick, and unnecessary roughness. The offending player is sent to a penalty box for two minutes for a minor infraction and five minutes for a major one. Teams may not substitute for their penalized players during the penalty. No team can be at more than a two-player disadvantage at a time. A team with a one- or two-player advantage is said to have the power play.

Women's Ice Hockey

Women's ice hockey was a demonstration sport at the 1998 Games in Nagano, Japan, and will be a full-medal sport at the 2002 Games. This is a rapidly-growing sport among girls and women, and they are one of the fastest-growing groups among USA Hockey membership registrations.

Women's Rules

Both the men's and the women's games are essentially the same. The most significant difference between the two is that women's ice hockey does not allow body checking at any level. Body checking is when a player uses the hip or shoulder to slow or stop an opponent who has control of the puck. Players may use the body to "ride" another player off the puck, but direct and intentional checking will be called for a penalty. The no-check rule allows players to concentrate on the skills of hockey—skating, passing, stickhandling, and shooting. Women also wear the same basic protective equipment as men, but girls and women are encouraged to wear female shoulder/chest pads and pelvic protectors.

©1988 USOC

JUDO

Judo is a popular wrestling form developed from jujitsu in 1882 by Jigoro Kano, a Japanese educator. Like jujitsu, it attempts to turn an attacker's force to one's own advantage. Considering judo uses holds, chokes, throws, trips, joint locks, kicks, and *atemi* (strikes to vital body areas), it is hard to believe that its name comes from the Japanese word *Ju* meaning "gentle." Judo is a discipline practiced today by over six million Japanese and many more athletes worldwide. Judo was first included in the Olympic Games in 1964.

Scoring

All scoring and refereeing terms are in Japanese. During a contest, for either men or women, a *judoka* (a person who practices the art of judo) may record an *ippon* (full-point), a *waza-ari* ("almost" *ippon*, a half of a point), a *yuko* ("almost" *waza-ari*, a quarter of a point), and a *koka* ("almost" *yuko*, an eighth of a point). There are negative scores too, resulting from *hansoku-make* (very grave infringements), *keikoku* (grave infringements), *chui* (serious infringements), and *shido* (slight infringements). The negative scores are recorded in favor of the contestant who did not commit the violation.

Competition

A judo match is won by the first to score an *ippon* or its equivalent, which is the sum of two *waza-ari*, known as an *awaste ippon*. A judoka earns an *ippon* by throwing his opponent to the mat (or *tatame*) with considerable force or speed, maintaining a hold for 30 seconds, applying armbar (elbow-joint-locking) techniques, or choking the rival while avoiding any action that might injure the neck or spine. (It is not allowed to put a lock on any bodily joint other than the elbow, as this could seriously injure the opponent.) An *awaste ippon* is earned by successfully executing one of the throwing techniques, which is given a *waza-ari*, followed by a 25-second hold-down, or vice versa, or by winning a *waza-ari* at the same time the opponent received a *keikoku*. If neither contestant is able to do this within the time limit, then a decision is rendered by the referee and two judges based on who demonstrated the better judo technique. Any lesser scores earned are counted toward the decision.

Judo is divided into weight categories much like boxing. For the Sydney Olympic Summer Games they were extra lightweight, half lightweight, lightweight, half middleweight, middleweight, half heavyweight, and heavyweight.

©1988 USOC

LUGE

Luge has been a popular sport in Europe since the late nineteenth century. Competitors slide down a twisting, ice-covered course while lying on their backs with their feet at the front of a runnered sled-like vehicle, called a luge. Competitors race against the clock, and the lowest combined time determines the winner. Luge has been an event of the Winter Olympic Games since 1964, with medals given in men's and women's singles and men's pairs.

Competition

Luge courses are constructed specially for the sport. They feature a number of standard turns and curves as well as straight stretches. A luge sled must conform to very specific rules regarding weight and size. Lugers strive to improve their speed by creating as little air resistance as possible by lying down in the most aerodynamic position possible. The head is held back, feet are kept pointed, and a skin-tight rubberized speedsuit is worn.

Techniques

Relaxation—relaxing the body is critical, but is a very difficult discipline to master. Being tense causes the sled to stiffen, cutting into the ice, instead of gliding over it. When relaxed, the slider absorbs vibration, keeping the blades on the ice and improving control and speed. Directional control of the luge requires very precise movements of the upper and lower body.

Leg steering—this causes the most loss of speed, so drivers prefer to shoulder steer as much as possible. However, for the sake of speed, it is best not to steer at all. Leg steering is achieved by pressing down and in on the end of the runner with the leg. Steering with the left leg causes the sled to veer right.

Shoulder steering—by pressing down with a shoulder, the bow in the side of the sled moves back, causing the bow on the other side to lead. The sled will move with the side with the bow farther back. Pressing the right shoulder causes the sled to track to the right.

Head steering—by rolling the head, slight pressure can be applied to one side of the sled, causing the same action to occur as with shoulder steering.

Handle steering—by pulling on a handle, the sled can be muscled to turn; however, the reaction time is slow. Olympic competitors use it only for an emergency.

MODERN PENTATHLON

The presumption is that modern pentathlon is called "modern" because Baron de Coubertin, who conceived of the first modern Olympics in 1896, also developed the first Olympic pentathlon and introduced it to the Games in 1912. To do that, he drew on the past, emphasizing the skills theoretically required of army couriers for survival and success in times of war in the early 1800s.

The basic premise behind the modern pentathlon is that a soldier is ordered to deliver a message. He starts out on the back of an unfamiliar horse, but is forced to dismount and fight a duel with swords. He escapes, but is trapped and has to shoot his way out with a pistol. Then he swims across a river, and finally he finishes his assignment by running 3,000 meters through the woods. The danger of an ambush may be long past, but skill, exertion, and endurance are all required to finish this event.

Scoring

Points are added or subtracted against a par of 1,000 points for each event except equestrian, which has a maximum of 1,100. The athlete with the highest overall point total after the five events wins the gold medal. The team score consists of the scores of the top three athletes from each nation.

Competition

All five events—shooting, fencing, swimming, equestrian, and running, in that order—are contested in one day. All five disciplines are the same for men and women and are held in the same order. The shooting competition has the athletes fire 20 shots at targets 10 meters away using, 4.5mm pistols. Athletes have 40 seconds to fire each shot, which is worth 10 target points. A perfect score is 200 target points. Fencing competitors use épée swords in bouts of no more than one minute. The winner of a bout is the first to score a hit in the target area, which is the whole body. An electronic tip at the end of the sword registers hits. If there are no hits, both fencers lose. Scoring is based on the percentage of wins. In the swimming competition, athletes swim a 200-meter freestyle. Point totals are based on times, and swimmers are placed in heats and lanes based on their personal-best times from the preceding season. The show-jumping equestrian event requires the athletes to ride an unfamiliar horse over an unfamiliar 350-400-meter course that has twelve jumps. Horses ridden are drawn by lot from a pool of one horse for every two competitors. The athlete with the highest cumulative point total from the first three events has first draw of the horses and rides first. The 3,000-meter run is the final event of the day-long competition. The leader through the first four events starts first, and this staggered start is achieved by converting every two-point differential in the total score of the first four events into a half-second difference. The order in which the athletes finish in the run determines the final standings.

©1988 USOC

ROWING

The style and rhythm of the rower's strokes are a series of clearly distinguishable actions that reflect a pattern of continuous movement and fluid motion. When the oars are brought out of the water, all should be at the same height, just above the surface, creating minimal splash. Although this gives the illusion of effortless motion, competitive rowing actually leaves muscles aflame, and bodies drained of oxygen and energy.

The power for the stroke is supplied by the rower's strong legs as well as upper body strength. The sliding seat also helps to generate great power through the rower's legs and feet. This entire sequence of rhythmical, balanced movements is repeated from 32 to 40 times per minute, depending on conditions, strategy, and length of the race. Amazingly, a world-class single sculler can move along at more than 10 miles per hour, and a men's eight can generate more than 13 miles per hour.

Categories

Boats compete in two basic categories: sculling and sweep rowing. Both men's and women's races are rowed on a 2,000-meter course no matter what the event.

In sweep rowing, two, four, or eight crew members sit facing the stern of the boat, each rower pulling one oar. With eight rowers and in some of the pairs and fours events, the vessel is steered by a non-rowing coxswain (pronounced "cox-n") who sits in the stern of the boat, facing the crew. The job of the coxswain is to steer the boat, decide tactics, and establish and maintain the speed and rhythm of the strokes of the rowers.

In sweep-rowing events without a coxswain, the boats may be steered by pressure exerted by the rowers or by rudder.

The other form of rowing, in which no coxswain is used, is called sculling, or scull racing. It is performed singly, by a pair, or by four rowers. Each rower (or sculler) faces the stern and pulls a pair of oars.

Competition

Olympic racing employs a double-elimination system, whereby each rower/crew gets at least two chances to compete. Competitors go through a series of elimination heats until only six crews/boats remain for the finals.

SAILING

Until recently, Olympic sailing was called yachting. The first boats designed solely for pleasure and sport were commissioned by the Dutch in the seventeenth century. The word yacht is an English derivation of the Dutch word "haght," meaning the small, fast cargo boats used in Holland during the fifteenth century.

Each sailing event is a series of races, called a regatta. There are some exclusively for men, some for women, and some open to both. The boats race either a windward return, a race starting into the wind and then returning to the start with the wind, or the trapezoidal course, which is a four-leg course starting and finishing in different places.

Classes

Finn—The Finn uses a centerboard dinghy and a one-man crew. Boats are assigned at random, but the helmsman provides his own sail and mast.

Tornado—The Tornado is a two-man catamaran, the fastest of all Olympic classes. Contributing to its speed is the large sail area and low weight.

470—The 470 is a two-man fiberglass craft that is 15.4 feet (470 cm) long. Like the Flying Dutchman, it uses a centerboard dinghy and a trapeze.

49er—The 49er is the newest class to race in the Olympics, having made its debut in the 2000 Sydney Games. The 49er has a two-man crew and is known for its speed.

Laser—The Laser is a fast, lightweight, one-person sailboat. The Laser debuted at the 1996 Atlanta Games and is an open class, allowing both men and women to compete.

Mistral—The Mistral replaced the *Lechner Division II Sailboard* after the 1992 Barcelona games. These sailboards are made of fiberglass, measure 12 feet 2 inches long, weigh 34.2 pounds, and have a sail area of 79.6 square feet.

Soling—The Soling is a keelboat and is the longest and heaviest of the classes. It is the only three-handed sailboat in Olympic competition.

Star—The Star class is a long, shallow boat with an enormous 285-square-foot (26.5 sq m) sail area. It's tough to sail in heavy seas and requires its crew to be strong and fit.

Europe—The Europe is the only single-handed women's Olympic boat and is considered very difficult to handle. The boat is adjustable to the sailor's height, weight, and experience.

SHOOTING

Target shooting with firearms dates back to the fourteenth century, but the weapons of that time were undependable and inaccurate. Over the centuries, weapons and ammunition have steadily improved, resulting in higher standards of accuracy and reliability. Target shooting was so popular in the nineteenth century that a shooting competition was included in the first modern Olympic Games in 1896.

Competition

Seventeen events in shooting were scheduled for the Sydney Games—six for shotguns, five with pistols, and six with rifles. Three relatively new events were the men's 10-meter running target and the men's and women's double trap.

Men's Events

Rapid-fire Pistol, 25 meters. This two-day event involves three phases. In the first phase, the shooter, using a .22-caliber pistol, has 8 seconds to fire at the 5 targets placed 25 meters away. He is allowed one shot per target. In the second phase, he has 6 seconds to fire at the same 5 targets. In the third phase, he has only 4 seconds in which to fire.

Free Pistol, 50 meters. The .22-caliber free pistol event allows shooters 2 1/2 hours to fire 60 shots at a target 50 meters away. The 10 ring, or bull's-eye, is only 5 cm (2 in) in diameter. Points for hits range from 10 in the center to 1 point on the outermost ring. The highest point total wins.

Smallbore Rifle, Prone Position, 50 meters. Competitors have 1 3/4 hours to take 60 shots using a .22-caliber rifle weighing up to 8 kg (17.6 lb). The shooter is lying flat on his stomach, one leg straight, the other bent, with his wrist at least 15 cm (6 in) above the ground. His 10-ring target has a bull's-eye which is a mere 1.6 cm (.625 in) in diameter.

Smallbore Rifle, Three Position, 50 meters. This most difficult event requires each competitor to shoot from 3 different positions: prone, kneeling, and standing. Shooters fire at a 10-ring target with a 1.6 cm (.625 in) bull's-eye, 50 meters away, using a .22-caliber rifle which can weigh up to, but not exceed, 8 kg (17.6 lb).

Air Rifle, 10 meters. Aiming at a bull's-eye only 0.5 millimeter in diameter 10 meters away, shooters fire one shot per target from the standing position. Both men and women use air- or gas-powered .177-caliber rifles, weighing up to 5.5 kg (12.1 lb).

Air Pistol, 10 meters. Men have 2 3/4 hours to take 60 shots at 10 meters. The bull's eye of the small 10-ring target is a scant 1 millimeter in diameter. Shooters use an air- or a gas-powered .177-caliber pistol, taking only one shot per target.

Running Game Target, 50 meters. This moving target event uses a life-size paper image of a wild boar as its target. The "boar," marked with a series of scoring rings ranging in point value from 1 to 10, runs along a 10-meter track at two speeds, normal and rapid. The shooter, using a .177-caliber air rifle with telescopic sights, is permitted 30 shots at each speed.

Men's Running Target, 10 meters. Sixty shots are fired at a target 10 meters away with a center ring of 5.5mm (.22 in) in diameter. Thirty shots are in a slow round and 30 in a rapid round. For the slow round, the target—pulled across an aisle that is 2 meters wide —is visible for five seconds. For the rapid round, the target is visible for two and one-half seconds.

Men's Double Trap. This event was contested for the second time in an Olympic Summer Games, having appeared first at Atlanta in 1996. Shotguns are fired from five adjacent shooting stations, each of which throws two targets from an underground bunker at speeds up to 50 mph. Competitors fire one shot per target, which weighs 105 g (3.7 oz), measures 11cm (4 in) in diameter, and is 25-26mm (less than 1 inch) thick.

Women's Events

Air Rifle, 10 meters. Shooters have 90 minutes to fire 40 shots from a standing position at a stationary target 10 meters away. The bull's eye is 0.5 millimeter in diameter. Women use air- or gas-powered .177-caliber rifles, weighing up to 5.5 kg (12.1 lb).

Smallbore Rifles, Three Positions, 50 meters. Women fire .22-caliber rifles, not exceeding 5.5 kg (12.1 lb). They shoot 40 rounds from each of three positions: prone, kneeling, and standing at a stationary target.

Sport Pistol, 25 meters. This event, using a .22-caliber standard pistol, is divided into two 30-shot stages. The "precision" stage uses a target with a 5 cm (2 in) bull's-eye. In 6 rounds, shooters have 6 minutes to fire 5 shots. In the "rapid-fire" stage the target has a 10 cm (4 in) bull's-eye which faces the shooter for 3 seconds, then mechanically turns away for 7 seconds.

Air Pistol, 10 meters. This event was added at the 1988 Games. Using an air- or gas-powered pistol, shots are taken at a small 10-ring stationary target. Shooters take one shot per target and have 90 minutes to complete 40 shots.

Women's Double Trap. This event was contested for the second time in an Olympic Summer Games, having made its debut at the Atlanta Games in 1996. Shotguns are shot from five adjacent shooting stations, each of which throws two targets from an underground bunker at speeds up to 50 mph. Competitors fire one shot per target, which is shot from one of three trap machines at each station. The combined score from the preliminary round and the finals determines the order of finish.

Mixed Events

Trap Shooting. Shooters use a 12-gauge shotgun. In competition, 10 cm (4 in) clay saucers, known as "clay pigeons," are dispatched mechanically at heights ranging from 1 to 4 meters above ground level. Each shooter has two shots. The clay pigeons are mechanically flung into the air, one to a shooter, at slightly different angles. Over three days, each shooter has 200 pigeons.

Skeet Shooting. This event also uses the 12-gauge shotgun and clay pigeons; however, sometimes two pigeons are released at a time, and the shooter is required to break both clays before either falls to the ground. Competitors move around to eight different stations.

The pigeon is released from one of two skeet towers located on either side of the shooting station and placed approximately 46 meters away. One tower is high, the other low, and a shooter never knows the angle or exact height of the next pigeon.

©1988 USOC

SKIING

Using equipment to travel over snow is an ancient practice. Greek historians mention skins, sliders, and shoes used for this purpose. Similar references occur in Norse myths. The earliest skis of which any record exists were found in bogs in Sweden and Finland. They are thought to be between 4,000 and 5,000 years old and are made of elongated curved frames covered with leather. Skis distribute the wearer's weight over a large area, preventing the skier from sinking into the snow.

Three kinds of skiing have developed: Alpine, Nordic, and freestyle. In Alpine, or downhill, skiing, victory belongs to the fastest skier down the mountain. Nordic, or cross-country, skiing is a race over relatively level surfaces along prearranged courses. (An important subcategory of Nordic ski races is ski jumping,, or movement down a vertical surface culminating in flight with the distance jumped and the skier's form being evaluated.) Freestyle skiing is a more recent event involving two separate competitions: moguls and aerials. Snowboarding has also been added as an Olympic event.

Equipment

Skis are made of strips of shaped wood, metal, or synthetic material and attached to a ski boot that is specially designed for a particular type of skiing. The hard, resistant surface of the skis is maintained by applying special ski waxes. The length of the skis depends upon the skier's height; however, downhill skis are shorter and wider than the ones used for cross country. Ski poles are made of light metal tubing with handgrips and straps, with a small disk at the bottom that allows a firm hold in the snow.

Alpine Skiing

There are four types of downhill races. The starting order is critical because the course deteriorates and becomes rutted under the pounding of the skis. There are five events in the Olympic Alpine program, with men and women competing separately in each.

Downhill

The goal is to descend the slope in the fastest possible time. This requires balance and coordination as speeds of 80 miles per hour are often reached. There are high-speed straights, sweeping curves, tight turns, and, at points, the skiers even become airborne over humps in the course. The skier must follow a series of gates, made up of poles with marker flags and placed in pairs. The racer must pass these gates; however, knocking down a pole does not matter as long as the racer has passed through the gate. Each competitor gets to make one run against the clock, and the differences among the top performers are often within hundredths of a second.

Slalom

A second type of Alpine racing is the slalom (Norwegian for "sloping track"). This, too, is essentially a downhill course, but it involves zigzagging down and across the surface of the slope. Each skier is required to weave in and out of a series of gates marked with blue- and red-flagged double poles. There are two separate runs on different courses, and the fastest combined time for the two runs establishes the winner.

Giant Slalom

The giant slalom is similar to the slalom except that it is steeper, faster, and longer, and the gates are farther apart. It combines the control and precision of slalom with the speed and daring of downhill. The race has two runs with the best combined time determining the winner.

Super Giant Slalom

The super giant slalom is a combination of downhill and giant slalom. Long, sweeping, high-speed turns make this event popular with spectators. Endurance, strength, and the ability to select the fastest, most direct line are determining factors in the "Super G." Like the downhill, there is only one run in this race.

Alpine Combined

The Alpine combined is a search for the best all-around skier. Competitors race separate downhill and slalom slopes with a single run over each course. The skier with the fastest combined time wins the event.

Nordic Skiing

Cross Country

Cross-country skiing places greater emphasis on strength and endurance, with less of an emphasis on speed. Courses are set up with colored markers, so that competitors follow the same route. The fundamental cross-country stride combines a kickoff step with one foot and a gliding step with the other. This is called "striding and gliding" with each step alternating smoothly and rapidly. The ski pole in one hand is planted down as the opposite leg begins its kickoff. Several variations to this basic stride allow for upward and downward movement and provide for some degree of rest from continuous exertion.

> *Waxing is a critical element in cross-country racing. It is estimated that some skiers use as many as a dozen different waxes and other preparations to prepare the soles of their skis for varying snow conditions.*

Ski Jumping

Ski jumpers race down a prepared vertical surface to a takeoff point, where the ultimate goal is to achieve a jump that displays a powerful takeoff, motionless control during flight, and a precise landing. The distance of the jump is measured from the lip of the takeoff to the place where the jumper's skis touch the snow on landing. Success in jumping depends more on the skier's balance and coordination than simply on the skier's jumping ability.

Jumps are scored by five judges. Points are given both for the distance of the jump and for style of execution. Up to 60 points are awarded for style, with an additional 60 points awarded to jumpers reaching the K point of the hill, which is the end of the steepest part of the landing slope. The highest and lowest scores are dropped and the points awarded by the remaining three judges are added together. Each contestant takes two jumps.

Deductions are made for ineffective takeoffs, improper positioning of body weight during flight (either too backward or too forward), skis being held at an improper angle, lack of stability or symmetry in flight, and for bent knees, hips, or back during flight. For landings, judges can deduct a maximum of five points. Faults can include failure to execute a *Telemark* landing (that is, with one leg straight and back and the other bent at the knee), insufficient or overbending of the knees upon landing, skis too wide apart, or any seeming instability, such as touching the snow with the hands on landing. An automatic deduction of 10 points occurs if a jumper falls; however, if he only touches the snow and regains his balance, the points deducted may be between 2 and 8 points.

Nordic Combined .

The Nordic combined event pairs ski jumping with cross-country ski racing. It is a two-day event, with ski jumping on the first day, cross country on the second. On the first day, each contestant makes three jumps with the best two sets of marks being combined for the score. The jumping scores are used to determine starting times for the second day's cross-country race. The competitor with the highest score starts first, with the others starting according to their standings in the jumping event. The team event is similar; however, the cross-country section consists of a relay race.

Freestyle Skiing

Freestyle skiing is made up of two separate competitions: moguls and aerials.

Moguls is an event that consists of carefully calculated high-speed turns on a heavily snow-bumped slope. The competitor is judged on speed and on the quality and technique of turns and upright aerials.

In aerial competition, a trained skier completes an acrobatic leap from a specially prepared ski jump. Scoring is based on the takeoff, form, and execution of the maneuver in the air, and landing. There are two types of competition aerials: upright, which is an acrobatic leap where the athlete's head does not move below the feet, and inverted, in which the contestant actually flips and twists. Jumps are scored on takeoff, form, execution of the maneuver, and landing, with scores multiplied by the degree of difficulty.

Snowboarding

Snowboarding is a young sport, barely thirty years old. It was a demonstration sport at the 1994 Olympic Winter Games and became a full-medal sport in the 1998 Games at Nagano, Japan.

Equipment

A snowboard resembles a short, fat Alpine ski with a tip, tail, edge, binding, camber, and base. However, a snowboard has a dings where the back foot rests when it is not in the back binding. Snowboards also have shovels and kicks at both ends. The kick (or rise) lifts the board to the top of the snow; the shovel is the upward curve of the board. Snowboards are made with a wood or foam core (and sometimes aluminum) with layers of other materials on top. They have soft or hard flexibility—hard boards are for racers and heavier people, while softer boards are used for freestyle snowboarding and lighter weight people. Every snowboard has a leash that attaches the snowboarder's front leg to the front binding. This keeps the board from snowboarding away by itself and causing serious problems for others on the slope. Snowboarding boots and bindings, like snowboards, are available in hard and soft styles, depending on the type of snowboard and the style of snowboarding an athlete chooses. Waxing the board regularly is necessary to keep it in top-notch shape for competitions.

Competition

Snowboarding is not a team sport. Instead, individuals enter in either of two events: the giant slalom and the half-pipe.

The Events

Giant Slalom

This event is snowboarding down a symmetrical giant slalom course, complete with gates. The snowboarder reaches incredible speeds and needs to be excellent at going through the gates. There is only one chance, so preparation is crucial to doing well in this event.

Half-pipe

This event takes its name from the shape of the course—a cylinder cut lengthwise. Snowboarders increase speed on the sloped portion, then go above the rim to demonstrate maneuvers such as jumps and rotations.

The winners are determined by the total number of points received in five categories: technique, height, rotation, landing, and technical merit.

©1988 USOC

SOCCER

Soccer is known throughout most of the world as "football." It is the most widely played team game in the world and the most popular spectator sport, followed avidly by hundreds of millions of fans. No sport has roused such passions. The outcome of at least one soccer match helped precipitate a shooting war. In 1969, Honduras and El Salvador went to war after a hotly contested World Cup match between the two countries.

Soccer is the only Olympic sport other than boxing to impose a maximum age restriction. All but three players, amateur or professional, on each team must be under the age of twenty-three.

The Game

The basic objective of the game is for one team to force a round leather ball, 68-70 cm in circumference—by kicking it or propelling it with the chest or head—into the opponent's goal. The goal mouth is 7.32 meters (24 ft) wide and 2.44 meters (8 ft) high, spanned by a crossbar and backed by netting. One point is awarded for each goal scored. The winning team is the one with the highest number of points. The game is played in 45-minute halves. If regulation time ends in a tie, an overtime period may be played. If the teams remain tied at the conclusion of overtime, the game may be decided by a kicking contest in which each team has up to five unobstructed—except for the goalkeeper—attempts to put the ball in the opponent's goal.

The goalkeeper is the only player on the team who may use his hands or arms to touch the ball. The other ten may kick it with their feet, block it with their torsos, or strike it with their heads, *but they may not use their hands.* The only exception is when the ball is put back into play from out of bounds.

The penalty for using the hands or arms to move the ball is to give the opponent a direct free kick. If this foul is committed in the penalty area, the kick is executed from a spot 11 meters from the goal mouth with only the goalkeeper defending the shot. For other infringements, such as deliberate obstruction of other players, an indirect free kick is awarded to the opposition. This does not, however, count toward a goal until the ball has been touched by another player. The referee may also assess other penalties, warning players for foul play, and if necessary removing them from the game.

Only two substitutions are permitted, per side, per game. If the two substitutions are used and a player is later injured, the team must play short.

©1988 USOC

SOFTBALL

Women's softball was a new event at the Olympic Summer Games at Atlanta in 1996 and was again an official medal sport at Sydney in 2000. However, hitting round objects with sticks or clubs (later named bats) has a history as a form of recreation that stretches back many centuries to the ancient Egyptians, Greeks, and Romans, as well to as the Aztec Indians of the fifteenth century. In the United States, softball began as an organized indoor sport late in the nineteenth century with rules, regulations, and a playing field that was designed to fit inside a gymnasium. That is why the distances between the bases and the pitcher's rubber are shorter than those for baseball.

The Playing Field

The softball playing field has the same outlines as those used in baseball, except the distance between the base paths for Olympic fast pitch softball is 60 feet rather than 90. This gives softball players much less distance than baseball players to work in, and they must react far more quickly. The distance from the pitcher to home plate is 40 feet (46 feet for the men's game). Outfield fences have minimum and maximum distances of 200 and 250 feet for women, 225 and 250 feet for men. There is no pitcher's mound or elevation. Instead, the pitcher works from a pitching rubber, or pitcher's plate, within a circle with a radius of 8 feet. The distance from the rubber to home plate is 40 feet in women's fast pitch softball.

The Game

Nine players comprise a fast pitch softball team: pitcher, catcher, first, second, and third basemen, shortstop, and left, center, and right fielders. (There are ten players on a slow pitch team, with the tenth covering the area behind second and third bases and the left and center outfields.) A regulation softball game is seven innings long and is scored the same as baseball—runners move around the bases from first base to home plate. Every time a runner crosses home plate, that's one run for her team. Olympic rules require that the ball be thrown by the pitcher underhand, but with windmill-style delivery. Before the pitcher delivers the pitch, both feet must be on the ground and inside the length of the pitcher's plate. For men, the pivot foot must contact the pitcher's plate and the non-pivot foot can be on or behind the plate. For women, both feet must be in contact with the pitcher's plate. The pitcher takes a signal from the catcher, holds the ball in both hands—but not for longer than ten seconds—and must make certain that the catcher is in position. As soon as one hand is taken off the ball, the pitch begins. Pitchers are not allowed to change their minds once the pitch begins. Fast pitch softball games usually feature strong pitchers, and as a result are often low-scoring pitching duels.

Equipment

The International Joint Rules Committee of the International Softball Federation (ISF) sets the standards for softballs internationally. In fast pitch Olympic competitions, softballs must be white and of a flat-seam style, with at least 88 white stitches. Official bats are constructed from one piece of hardwood, with the grain of the wood running parallel. Bats made from metal, plastic, an aluminum alloy, or other man-made material are acceptable as well. All bats, whether wood or metal, require a safety grip (10 to 15 inches long) and carry an "Official Softball" label.

©1988 USOC

SPEEDSKATING

Speed races can be traced to the beginning of the seventeenth century in the Netherlands. Races were being held on the North American continent by the early 1800s, and they quickly became a favorite sport in the northern United States and Canada. Speedskating competitions were held at the first Olympic Winter Games at Chamonix, France, in 1924.

Speedskating has been divided into two sections—short track and long track—with separate events for each. Starting positions for all races are left to the luck of the draw.

Short Track

Short-track skating begins with a mass start with four to six competitors lining up for the heat. They skate on a short 111-meter oval track for varying distances and compete in several elimination heats. The first one across the finish line is the winner, and the top two finishers in a heat progress to the next run.

Unlike the longer-distance speedskating events, short-track speedskating is much faster paced with frequent falls. The lead skater has the right of way, and anyone passing the lead has the responsibility to pass cleanly, without body contact. A body contact infraction is cause for disqualification and can lead to falls. Many of the falls and body contact are caused by the tight corners on the small track where skaters tend to pile up. To minimize participant injury, boards surrounding the track are draped with crash pads.

Aside from being in superb shape, short-track speedskaters must be agile and have quick reaction times to be successful.

Long Track

In long-track speedskating, competitors race in pairs around a 400-meter track. While the two skaters may appear to be racing each other, they are actually racing against the clock and against a time established by a previous skater in a previous heat.

Many longtime observers feel that in long-track speedskating, the key to an outstanding performance is in consistently timed laps. Skaters keep themselves in a low crouched position to reduce air resistance and improve speed.

©1988 USOC

SWIMMING

Forty thousand people watched the first Olympic swimming contests that were held outdoors in open water. The weather had turned unusually cold at the Bay of Zea at Phaleron, near Piraeus, and on the morning of the competition the temperature in the water had dropped to 13 degrees Celcius (55 degrees Fahrenheit).

Early competitions were held in lakes, rivers, and the open sea, with swimmers competing not only against each other but against the currents, tides, bitter cold, and even 12-foot waves. All events are now held in Olympic-size pools 50 meters long (almost 55 yards) with a minimum of eight lanes, each from 7 to 9 feet (2 to 2.7 m) wide. The water temperature is regulated and must be kept at 25-27° C (77-80° F).

The Events

The events are categorized by the type of stroke the swimmer uses. Men and women compete separately, with the distances ranging from 50 meters to 1,500 meters for men, and from 50 meters to 800 meters for women.

The events included in the Olympic Games include:

Freestyle is where the competitor may swim any stroke he or she prefers, usually the Australian crawl, where the arms alternately come out of the water and the legs flutter kick.

Backstroke is essentially the crawl stroke but with the swimmer's back turned to the water. Swimmers must stay on their backs at all times.

Breaststroke is where all leg and arm movements must be made simultaneously. The hands must be pushed forward together and from the breast, and must be brought back on or under the surface of the water. Only the backward and out frog-leg kick is allowed.

Butterfly was originally a variation of the breaststroke. The breaststroke had always been a controversial stroke because of ongoing arguments as to what constituted a legal or illegal technique. In the early 1940s some U.S. swimmers discovered a "loophole" in the rules then in force and began to bring their arms back above the surface of the water, saving time and energy. In 1952, this new technique was officially recognized as the fourth Olympic swimming style and given its own set of competitions, separate from the breaststroke.

Individual Medley comprises all four of the above competitive strokes in one race; the order of the strokes is butterfly, backstroke, breaststroke, and freestyle.

Medley Relay is an event swum by a team of four, with each member swimming one leg (one portion or quarter) of the relay. The race is swum in the order of backstroke first, then breaststroke, butterfly, and freestyle.

Freestyle Relay is where each swimmer chooses the stroke he or she will use, with each leg of the race swum by a different team member. As in the medley relay, no individual may swim more than one leg of the event.

The Race

The race is ready to begin when the swimmers are called to the starting position by the starter, who visually makes certain that all swimmers are down and still. Once the starter is satisfied, the race is started by an electronic tone. The race will be recalled if the starter feels that one of the swimmers has "jumped the gun," and the swimmers will get ready to start the race again. A competitor will be disqualified for causing a second premature start.

Starts and turns are key points of any race; many a race has been lost by a swimmer who starts or turns poorly.

Quick turns are essential to a good race. Swimmers must touch the wall in turning in all events; however, in the freestyle and the backstroke, the swimmer may somersault at the wall, touching it only with the feet. In the other two competitive strokes, both hands must touch the wall before the turn can be executed.

There are basically two ways to swim a distance race of 200 meters or more. Some swim it evenly, holding the same pace throughout the entire race. Others employ the "negative split" by swimming the second half of a race faster than the first.

Many male swimmers will shave their arms, legs, chest, and back—and some, even their head—right before the meet to lessen water resistance and increase their speed.

SYNCHRONIZED SWIMMING

Synchronized swimming is a sport requiring power, strength, and technical skill. These artistically choreographed routines display overall body strength and agility, grace and beauty, split-second timing, musical interpretation, and a flair for the dramatic.

Maintaining an effortless appearance while performing a strenuous routine is very difficult, yet this is an important quality expected by the judges. The physical demands and endurance needed to perform the approximately four-minute routine are not much different from running for that same length of time.

Because approximately half of the swimmers' time is spent entirely underwater during competition, without contact with the bottom of the pool, swimmers run, bike, lap swim, and lift weights to build up endurance and strength.

They also spend hours every day practicing ballet and various forms of dance to develop the artistic expression and fluid, graceful movements that are essential to synchronized swimming.

Scoring

Competition is divided into two elements: compulsory figures and original routines. A panel of seven judges awards points from 0 to 10 based on the accuracy of the performance for the technical routine; technical merit and artistic impression are scored for the original routines.

Competition

Technical Routine Elements

The technical routine has a number of required elements that are performed in a set order, using the music of each competitor's choice. The time limit is 2 minutes, 50 seconds for the team competition and 2 minutes, 20 seconds for the duet competition. The times include a maximum of 10 seconds for movements on the deck before entering the water. Scores are the total of the technical merit and artistic impression awards. The highest and lowest awards for each one are canceled. Then each is divided by the number of judges minus two, and the technical merit award is multiplied by six and the artistic impression award is multiplied by four.

Except for the cadence action in the team competition, deck movements and entry into the water must be done simultaneously by each team member. Ten seconds (plus or minus) are the allotted time limits. For example, a technical routine in the team competition is satisfactory if its length is between 2 minutes, 40 seconds and 3 minutes.

Original Routine Competition

Original routine competition execution, synchronization, and difficulty are rated for the technical merit score, while the artistic impression score reflects choreography, musical interpretation, and the manner of presentation.

TABLE TENNIS

Table tennis was first played in England with improvised equipment on dining-room tables using small rubber and cork balls. By the 1900s, the game was very popular in the United States as well as in England. Early manufactured sets were called Gossimar, Whiff-Whaff, and, more commonly, Ping-Pong, the latter being a trade name. In 1922, its popularity as a parlor game waned while at the same time movements were starting to revive table tennis as a serious sport. Except for the similarity of equipment and basic scoring rules, there's a world of difference between table tennis at the Olympic level and the friendly household pastime.

Scoring

One player serves until 5 points have been scored, after which the opponent serves for the next 5 points. A game is won by the player who first scores 21 points. If, however, the score is tied at 20, play continues until one player gains a 2-point advantage, with the service changing after each point. A match consists of three games out of five.

Competition

Table tennis involves hitting a small celluloid ball back and forth over a net until one of the players misses the ball, hits it into the net, or hits it off the table. In each of these cases, the opponent scores a point. To serve, a player holds the ball on the flat, open palm of the hand, then throws it up and strikes it as it falls. The served ball must first hit the table on the server's side of the net, then bounce to the other side of the net, hitting the table before being returned by the other player. When a serve touches the net but is otherwise a good serve, it is called a "let" and replayed. Players rotate ends after every game and when one player reaches 10 in the deciding game of the match.

Balls in play that touch either the net or the table edge are valid shots. When, in the opinion of the umpire, a ball hits the side of the table rather than the edge, the player who made the shot loses the point.

In doubles play, service must be from the right-hand court into the opponent's right-hand court, and partners must alternate hitting the ball. The sequence of one specific partner hitting to one specific opponent must be changed after each game and when one side reaches 10 in the deciding game of the match.

TAEKWONDO

Paintings of taekwondo practitioners have been found on the ceiling of at least one royal tomb from the Koguryo dynasty (about 50 B.C.) of Korean history. The techniques depicted match those practiced today, not just in Korea, but around the world in at least 140 countries.

Taekwondo is a martial art that combines straight line and circular movements—from Japanese and Chinese styles, respectively—with a variety of kicking techniques using bare hands and feet. *Tae* means to kick or strike with the foot; *kwon* means fist or to strike with the hand; *do* means discipline or art or way. Thus, taekwondo is the art, or way, of kicking and punching. However, taekwondo is more than a sport because the practitioner learns to improve spiritually while becoming proficient in the sport.

A demonstration sport in the 1988 Games in Seoul and the 1992 Games in Barcelona, taekwondo emerged as a full-medal sport at the 2000 Games in Sydney.

Competition

A kick is a *cha-gi*, and there are several types:

- *ahp*: a front kick;
- *dolryo*: a round kick;
- *dwi*: a back kick;
- *guligi*: a hook kick;
- *twi-o*: a jumping kick; and
- *yop*: a side kick.

Kicks with the feet may be aimed at the head or body, but close-fisted punches may only be aimed at the body.

Men and women competed separately at Sydney in a single elimination format to decide the winner of the gold and silver medals. Anyone with one loss was moved to a separate bracket; the bronze medal winner was determined from here.

TENNIS

When tennis is played by two opponents, one per side, the game is known as singles. When the game is played in pairs, it is called doubles. Men and women compete separately in both singles and doubles competitions.

Scoring

The scoring in a tennis game goes by a sequence of four points, specified as 15, 30, 40, and game. The score of a player who does not have a point is referred to as "love." Four points wins the game, unless the score is tied at 40, at which time the first player to go ahead by two points wins the game. Any time the score is tied, from 40-40 on, the game is at "deuce."

The player who scores the next point, breaking the tie, is said to have the advantage, or "ad." If the server has the advantage, it's referred to as "ad in"; if the receiver is the one who scored, it is called "ad out." If the player who has the advantage scores the next point, the game is over. If the other player wins the point, the score returns to "deuce."

The score of the server is always given first, no matter who's leading. If the score is 15-30, the receiver is leading by a point. During a set, players exchange sides after each odd-numbered game starting with the first. This applies both to singles and doubles.

Competition

Six games wins a set, but just as a game must be won by two points, the margin of victory has to be two games. If the score is tied 6-6, a tie-breaking game is played unless it is the final set of a match (the third set for women; the fifth set for men). This match-deciding set continues indefinitely, until one competitor moves ahead by two games.

During regular play, serve alternates between the players after each game. In a tiebreaker, the first player serves one point, after which the serve is alternated after every second point. This continues indefinitely until someone reaches at least 7 points with a margin of 2.

Power serving has become an important aspect of winning tennis. Often a player's ability to win a game depends on the ability to "break service" (win a game that the opponent is serving).

TRIATHLON

Triathlons began as a different form of training for marathon and 10-kilometer, or 10K, runners who wanted a break in their regular training programs. Since 1978, when the first Ironman Triathlon was held in Hawaii, the sport has grown tremendously. In September 1994, the International Olympic Committee named triathlon as a medal sport for the 2000 Olympic Summer Games.

The Events

There are three events in the triathlon: a 1.5K swim, a 40K bike ride, and a 10K run. Both men and women compete in exactly the same events, but on separate days.

Scoring

There is no scoring, as such, in the triathlon. The clock starts as soon as the gun sounds for the first event—the swim. The three events are performed one after another, with no rest breaks or timeouts. The competitor who crosses the line first at the end of the swim, bike ride, and run wins the gold medal for the competition. All athletes need speed, strength, and endurance, of course, but strategy is just as important.

The Competition

1.5K Swim

The fastest swimmers tend to be in the lead, but slower swimmers often swim "on the toes" or in the draft of a faster swimmer. This strategy can keep them in the race. At the end of the swim, which takes place in open water, the athletes have to change from swim caps and goggles—or their wetsuits if the water temperature is below 20° C (68° F)—and get on their bicycles.

40K Bike

Triathletes must put on cycling helmets, but it is standard procedure to have shoes already attached to the bike pedals and to put them on as the athletes get up to speed on the course. Drafting—cycling behind another, faster competitor—is legal in an Olympic triathlon and saves energy.

10K Run

The final event of the triathlon—the 10K run—begins with another change of gear for the athletes. They get rid of their helmets, slide into running shoes, and are off for the last of the three events. There may be a surge during the run—runners trying to put distance between themselves and the other runners.

©1988 USOC

VOLLEYBALL

Although they have similar names and both involve hitting a ball over a net, volleyball and its offshoot, beach volleyball, have different rules. Each is a medal sport at the Summer Olympic Games.

Beach Volleyball

Beach volleyball began as a sport in the United States during the 1920s and became popular in California in 1947. The first World Championships were held in 1976, and twenty years later the sport became a medal event at the Atlanta Games.

The Game

Beach volleyball is played outside in the sand on a rectangle 59 feet (18 m) long by 29 1/2 feet (9 m) wide. The net dividing the rectangle is 8 feet (2.4 m) high for the men's game, but slightly lower for the women's game. Two teams of two players each compete against one another. The object of the game is to hit the ball back and forth across the net (with your hands or arms) in such a way that the opposing team cannot return it. The two players decide on the serving order and maintain it during the game. No substitutes, or coaching, are allowed during a match.

Scoring

After the ball is served, the opposing team gets three contacts with the ball before they must return it to the other team's side. This back and forth continues until the ball touches the sand, goes out of bounds, or a player commits a foul, e.g., steps under the net, touches the net, or goes out of bounds by the net. The team that wins this ad wins the right to serve or gets to hold service. Beach volleyball is played to 15 points, but the winning team must win by at least 2 points. Neither team is given a weather advantage—they change sides after every 5 points.

Volleyball

Volleyball was invented in 1895 as a recreational pastime by an American, William G. Morgan, physical education director of the Young Men's Christian Association chapter in Holyoke, Massachusetts. His game, which he originally called Mintonette, was treated as no more than casual recreation until American servicemen exported it during and after World War II to Asia and Europe. It quickly became popular not only in the United States, but around the world.

The Court

Volleyball is played indoors on a rectangular court 29 by 59 feet (9 x 18 m). The court is wood or a synthetic material and is divided by a net 7 feet, 11 5/8 inches (2.4 m) high for men and 7 feet, 4 1/8 inches (2.2 m) high for women. It cannot be less than 32 feet (9.7 m) long and 3 feet (.91 m) wide. Red and white antennas at both ends project 2.6 feet (80 cm) above the net. A ball is out of play if it hits the antenna, and any spikes or hits have to be inside the antennas to be in play. A serving line is at the back end of the court, and a player is allowed to serve from anywhere behind this back-end line. The ball has a circumference of 2.1 to 2.2 feet (65-67 cm), weighs 9-10 ounces (255-284 grams), and has a pressure of 4.5 to 6.0 pounds (2-2.7kg).

The Game

Each team has six players—left, center, and right forwards, who are in the frontcourt closest to the net, and left, center, and right backs, who line up in the backcourt directly behind their respective forwards. Points are scored by successfully landing the ball in the court of the opponent without its being returned. The ball is hit back and forth over the net, with the hands, fists, forearms, head, or any part of the body above the waist. The return over the net must be done without catching, holding, or carrying the ball; without a player's touching the net; and without entering the area of the opponent. Only three hits are allowed on a side before the ball goes over the net, and no player may strike the ball two times in a row.

Competition

Olympic volleyball matches follow a best-of-five format, with every play of every game counting as 1 point. Games 1 through 4 are played to 25 points, but the winner must win by 2 points. If a team is not ahead by 2 points when it reaches 25, the teams continue play until one team wins by 2 points. After four games, if the teams are tied two games apiece, the fifth game is played to 15 points, but still must be won by 2 points. This revamped scoring system has made the game quicker and easier to understand.

In addition to point-per-play scoring, a new defensive position— the libero—has been added. The libero wears a special jersey and substitutes at any time in the backcourt for a frontcourt player, but cannot serve or attack the ball. Libero specialists are passers and diggers and have been used to help their teams develop a precision offensive attack.

Traditional volleyball matches are decided on the best three out of five sets. A team wins a set when it scores 15 points, provided the margin is two or more points. If the leading team is not ahead by 2 points, play continues until one team has 17 points, regardless of the margin. During the first four games of any match, a point may be scored only by the team that is serving; a player continues to serve as long as his or her team continues to score points. If the defensive team wins a rally, it earns the right to serve. On a service shift, all members of the new serving team immediately rotate, moving clockwise one position. "Speed scoring" goes into effect if a fifth game is needed to decide a match. This means a team can score whether or not it is serving. For example, if one team faults on service, the receiving team scores a point in addition to winning the right to serve.

©1988 USOC

WATER POLO

Water polo originated in England during the 1870s, and as legend has it, the sport was developed by spirited young men who wanted to play rugby and cool off at the same time. It soon became popular in the United States and is now a major sport in a number of European countries. Its first appearance in the Olympics was at the 1900 Games, where it was the first team sport admitted to the Olympics.

Today, in the Olympic Games, women have their own water polo events, but the rules are the same as for men. There are relatively few male players under 6 feet tall, and most weigh at least 220 pounds. Women are correspondingly tall and well-muscled. Height is essential for a long reach, a definite advantage in passing and shooting, while heft and muscle enable the athlete to withstand the punishing demands of the game.

Competition

Games are divided into four periods of 7 minutes each, with a 2-minute interval between periods. One point is scored when the ball is thrown or shoved completely past the face of the goal. In case of a tie, two 3-minute overtime periods are held; if necessary a third, sudden-death overtime with no time limit is played.

Players wear caps of contrasting colors for easier identification; the official rules stipulate white for one team, blue for the other, and red caps for the goalies.

A water polo team consists of seven players: a goalkeeper and six field players. In addition, each team keeps six substitutes in reserve. With the exception of the goalkeeper, players must tread water the entire time, never touching the bottom or sides of the pool, nor may they take the ball beneath the surface of the water.

Each quarter is started with each team spread out along its own goal line. The referee throws the ball into the center of the pool and both sides rush to gain possession. The team that captures the ball then attempts to advance it toward the opponent's goal by passing it between teammates, who dribble it with their forearms. Players may move the ball with any part of their bodies, but may not use more than one hand at a time or use clenched fists. The team in possession only has 35 seconds to get off a shot.

WEIGHTLIFTING

When the modern Olympic Games began, weightlifting was one of the charter sports. There were no weight divisions at that time, and the first events were a one-handed lift and a two-handed lift.

Women were included in the weightlifting events for the first time at the 2000 Olympic Summer Games in Sydney.

Scoring

Each contestant is allowed three attempts at each selected weight of the two types of lift. Only the best lift from each event is counted toward the final combined score. A majority decision from three referees decides whether a lift is successful.

In both events, the bar must be held overhead until the referees' signal. The down signal is not given until the lifter is motionless and displays proper form.

When a tie occurs, the contestant with the lower body-weight is declared the winner. Often a champion will make a fourth attempt, which does not count as part of the competition but can count as a world record.

Competition

The lifts

Snatch—In executing the snatch, the contestant grasps the barbell and in one continuous forceful motion lifts it to the full extent of both arms over the head. The legs may be flexed or moved at any time during this lift, but must be returned to the same plane to complete the lift. The competitor must come to an erect position with arms locked. When the feet, body, and bar lie in the same plane, the referees give the down signal.

Clean and jerk—The clean and jerk involves lifting the barbell to shoulder level in one motion and above the head in another, separate motion. The lift is designed as two distinct efforts so the competitor can get the greatest weight overhead. For the "clean," the lifter must grip the bar and lift it as high as his or her power will allow, keeping it close to the body. Before the bar begins to drop, the lifter squats, secures the bar on the shoulders or chest, and then stands up straight. The "jerk" is the second effort, as the lifter thrusts the bar from its position on the body to a position overhead, again in one motion, and splits the legs front and back like an open scissors. Finally, the lifter brings the feet together and waits for the referees' down signal.

©1988 USOC

WRESTLING

Of the two styles of wrestling, Greco-Roman and freestyle, Greco-Roman is the classic form, the style of wrestling practiced in ancient Greece. Although differences in techniques are numerous, the most obvious is that Greco-Roman is confined to upper-body grappling. Freestyle, by contrast, involves the entire body, and leg attacks are permitted.

Greco-Roman matches involve classic throws in which a wrestler grasps his opponent above the waist and actually throws him over his head. Freestyle wrestlers use their legs to attack as well as to counter-attack, using moves such as a foot-sweep in which one wrestler attempts to take the other off his feet, or a simple leg grab with which leverage can be applied. Europeans tend to favor the Greco-Roman classical style, while North America's best wrestlers are attracted to the freestyle. United States collegiate wrestling, for example, is very similar to international freestyle. Today, the training and techniques of each style are so specialized that most wrestlers concentrate on one style or the other.

There are currently 16 different wrestling divisions in Olympic competition, 8 categories in each of the two styles. With respect to total medals available, wrestling is a prolific sport in the Olympics, offering 48 possible medals—16 gold, 16 silver, and 16 bronze.

Rules

The goal in wrestling is to "pin" an opponent within a circle marked out on a 12-square-meter mat. (At the 2000 Games the mat was cut off at the corners to form an octagon.) The competition area is a yellow circle 9 meters in diameter and 4-cm thick with a vinyl cover. The central wrestling area is a 7-meter yellow circle where most of the wrestling takes place. A central circle of 1 meter outlined in red within this larger circle is where the wrestlers begin their match. They return to this circle for *par terre* (literally, on the ground) when the referee tells them to.

A 1-meter red band on the outside of the central wrestling area marks the passivity zone. This area warns the wrestlers that they are close to the edge of the competition area. Finally, the entire circle has a blue border at least 1.5 meters wide known as the protection area.

The pin is comparable to a knockout in boxing, constituting an automatic victory. It is accomplished when one wrestler holds both his opponent's shoulders to the mat for a half-second. If no pin occurs, the victory goes to the wrestler who has gained the most points. The match ends earlier if one of the wrestlers builds a lead of 10 points.

Scoring

Freestyle

In freestyle, points may be earned for taking the opponent to the mat (1 point); gaining the upper position while on the mat

(1 point); touching an opponent's elbow, shoulder, or head to the mat (2 points); and taking an opponent directly from his feet to his back (3 points). There are many other legal offensive moves, but these are among the most dramatic.

Greco-Roman

In Greco-Roman wrestling, holds are permitted only above the waist. Spectacular throws are awarded the greatest number of points. These moves, which usually earn 3 points, are quite risky, even for the executor who must place himself in a vulnerable position just to achieve them. A fourth point may be earned in the throw for grand amplitude. It is essentially an appreciation point in recognition of the extra effort the throw requires.

Judging

A bout is controlled by four officials: mat chairman, judge, referee, and timekeeper. The referee oversees all action on the mat. Although no penalty points are subtracted for an illegal throw or hold, a wrestler may be disqualified for any move posing a physical danger to an opponent, e.g., choking, hitting, kicking, or biting. The referee also keeps the match moving along by calling the wrestlers to their feet if the bout appears to have reached an impasse.

Competition

A wrestling bout begins when the referee calls the wrestlers to the center of the mat. They are examined for correct attire, and the referee makes sure each has no oil or grease applied to his body (thereby making him slippery and hard to hold). The competitors retire to their respective corners until the referee whistles the start of the bout.

Each Olympic match lasts for two 3-minute periods. If necessary, the rules allow for one 3-minute overtime period per bout. A match is discontinued as the result of a fall or if one wrestler reaches a 10-point lead. If the time limit is reached without either a fall or a 10-point lead, the wrestler with the most points is pronounced the winner.

Both freestyle and Greco-Roman wrestling at the Olympic Games follow the same eight weight categories. Although women do not compete in Olympic wrestling at this time, it is possible that they may appear on the program for the 2004 Olympic Summer Games in Athens, Greece.

5

Olympic & Sports Organizations

The organization of, and participation in, the Olympic Games requires the cooperation of a number of independent organizations.

The International Olympic Committee (IOC)

The IOC is responsible for determining where the Games will be held. It is also the obligation of its membership to uphold the principles of the Olympic Ideal and Philosophy beyond any personal, religious, national, or political interest. The IOC is responsible for sustaining the Olympic Movement.

The members of the IOC are individuals who act as the IOC's representatives in their respective countries, not as delegates of their countries within the IOC. The members meet once a year at the IOC Session. They retire at the end of the calendar year in which they turn 70 years old, unless they were elected before the opening of the 110th Session (December 11, 1999). In that case, they must retire at the age of 80. Members elected before 1966 are members for life. The IOC chooses and elects its members from among such persons as its nominations committee considers qualified. There are currently 113 members and 19 honorary members.

The International Olympic Committee's address is—

Chateau de Vidy, CH-1007
Lausanne, Switzerland
Tel: (41-21) 621-6111   Fax: (41-21) 621-6216
www.olympics.org

The National Olympic Committees

Olympic Committees have been created, with the design and objectives of the IOC, to prepare national teams to participate in the Olympic Games. Among the tasks of these committees is to promote the Olympic Movement and its principles at the national level.

The national committees work closely with the IOC in all aspects related to the Games. They are also responsible for applying the rules concerning eligibility of athletes for the Games. Today there are more than 150 national committees throughout the world.

The U.S. Olympic Committee's address is—

Olympic House
One Olympic Plaza
Colorado Springs, CO 80909-5760
Tel: (719) 632-5551   Fax: (719) 578-6216
www.usoc.org

International Sports Federations

There are world or international federations for each individual sport, which coordinate sport activities in general throughout the world.

The addresses of sports federations follow—

National Archery Assn.
One Olympic Plaza
Colorado Springs, CO 80909
Tel: (719) 578-4576
Fax: (719) 632-4733
www.usarchery.org

U.S. Badminton Assn.
One Olympic Plaza
Colorado Springs, CO 80909
Tel: (719) 578-4808
Fax: (719) 578-4507
www.usabadminton.org

USA Baseball
2160 Greenwood Ave.
Trenton, NJ 08609
Tel: (609) 586-2381
Fax: (609) 587-1818
www.usabaseball.com

USA Basketball
5465 Mark Dabling Blvd.
Colorado Springs, CO 80918
Tel: (719) 590-4800
Fax: (719) 590-4811
www.usabasketball.com

U.S. Biathlon Assn.
421 Old Military Road
Lake Placid, NY 12946
Tel: (518) 523-3836
Fax: (518) 523-3889

U.S. Bobsled & Skeleton Federation
P.O. Box 828
(421 Old Military Road)
Lake Placid, NY 12946
Tel: (518) 523-1842
Fax: (518) 523-9491
www.usabobsledandskeleton.org

USA Boxing
One Olympic Plaza
Colorado Springs, CO 80909
Tel: (719) 578-4506
Fax: (719) 632-3426
www.usaboxing.org

American Canoe Assn.
7432 Alban Station Blvd.,
   Ste. B-226
Springfield, VA 22150
Tel: (703) 451-0141
Fax: (703) 451-2245
(For recreational programs)

U.S. Canoe & Kayak Team
Pan American Plaza, Ste. 610
201 South Capitol Ave.
Indianapolis, IN 46225
Tel: (317) 237-5690
Fax: (317) 237-5694
www.usacanoekayak.org

U.S. Curling Assn.
1100 Center Point Dr., Box 866
Stevens Point, WI 54481
Tel: (715) 344-1199
Fax: (715) 344-6885
www.usacurl.org

U.S. Cycling Federation
One Olympic Plaza
Colorado Springs, CO 80909- 5775
Tel: (719) 578-4581
Fax: (719) 578-4628 or
          (719) 578-4596
E-mail: usac@usacycling.org
www.usacycling.org

United States Diving, Inc.
Pan American Plaza, Ste. 430
201 South Capitol Ave.
Indianapolis, IN 46225
Tel: (317) 237-5252
Fax: (317) 237-5257
www.usadiving.org

American Horse Shows Assn.
4047 Iron Works Parkway
Lexington, KY 40511
Tel: (606) 258-2472
Fax: (606) 231-6662
E-mail: webmaster@ahsa.org
www.ahsa.org

U.S. Equestrian Team
Pottersville Road
Gladstone, NJ 07934
Tel: (908) 234-1251
Fax: (908) 234-9417

U.S. Fencing Assn.
One Olympic Plaza
Colorado Springs, CO 80909
Tel: (719) 578-4511
Fax: (719) 632-5737
www.USFencing.org

U.S. Field Hockey Assn.
One Olympic Plaza
Colorado Springs, CO 80909
Tel: (719) 578-4567
Fax: (719) 632-0979
www.usfieldhockey.org

U.S. Figure Skating Assn.
20 First Street
Colorado Springs, CO 80906
Tel: (719) 635-5200
Fax: (719) 635-9548
www.usfa.com

USA Gymnastics
Pan American Plaza, Ste. 300
201 South Capitol Ave.
Indianapolis, IN 46225
Tel: (317) 237-5050
Fax: (317) 237-5069
www.usa-gymnastics.org

USA Hockey
4965 North 30th Street
Colorado Springs, CO 80919
Tel: (317) 599-5500
Fax: (317) 599-5994
www.usahockey.com

U.S. Judo, Inc.
P.O. Box 10013
El Paso, TX 79991
Tel: (915) 565-8754
Fax: (915) 566-1668
www.usjudo.org

U.S. Luge Assn.
P.O. Box 651
Lake Placid, NY 12946
Tel: (518) 523-2071
Fax: (518) 523-4106
www.usluge.org

U.S. Modern Pentathlon Assn.
530 McCullough, Ste. 619
San Antonio, TX 78215
Tel: (210) 246-3000
Fax: (210) 246-3096
www.pentathlon.org

U.S. Rowing Assn.
Pan American Plaza, Ste. 400
201 South Capitol Ave.
Indianapolis, IN 46225
Tel: (317) 237-5656
Fax: (317) 237-5646
www.usrowing.org

U.S. Sailing Assn.

P.O. Box 209
Newport, RI 02840
Tel: (401) 849-5200
Fax: (401) 849-5208
www.ussailing.org

USA Shooting

One Olympic Plaza
Colorado Springs, CO 80909
Tel: (719) 578-4670
Fax: (719) 635-7989
www.usashooting.com

U.S. Skiing

P.O. Box 100
(1500 Kearns Blvd.)
Park City, UT 84060
Tel: (801) 649-9090
Fax: (801) 649-3613
www.usskiteam.com

U.S. Soccer Federation

U.S. Soccer House
1801-1811 S. Prairie Ave.
Chicago, IL 60616
Tel: (312) 808-1300
Fax: (312) 808-1301
www.us-soccer.com

Amateur Softball Assn.

2801 N.E. 50th Street
Oklahoma City, OK 73111-7203
Tel: (405) 424-5266
Fax: (405) 424-3855
E-mail: info@softball.org
www.usasoftball.com

U.S. Speedskating

P.O. Box 16157
Rocky River, OH 44116
Tel: (216) 899-0128
Fax: (216) 899-0109
www.usspeedskating.org

U.S. Swimming, Inc.

One Olympic Plaza
Colorado Springs, CO 80909
Tel: (719) 578-4578
Fax: (719) 578-4669
www.usa-swimming.org

U.S. Synchronized Swimming, Inc.

Pan American Plaza, Ste. 510
201 South Capitol Ave.
Indianapolis, IN 46225
Tel: (317) 237-5700
Fax: (317) 237-5705
www.usasynchro.org

USA Table Tennis

One Olympic Plaza
Colorado Springs, CO 80909
Tel: (719) 578-4583
Fax: (719) 632-6071
www.usatt.org

U.S. Taekwondo Union

One Olympic Plaza, Ste. 405
Colorado Springs, CO 80909
Tel: (719) 578-4632
Fax: (719) 578-4642
E-mail: mediaustu@aol.com
www.ustu.org

U.S. Team Handball Fed.

One Olympic Plaza
Colorado Springs, CO 80909
Tel: (719) 578-4582
Fax: (719) 475-1240
www.usateamhandball.org

U.S. Tennis Assn.

70 West Red Oak Lane
White Plains, NY 10604
Tel: (914) 696-7000
Fax: (914) 696-7167
www.usta.com

USA Track & Field

P.O. Box 120
Indianapolis, IN 46206
Tel: (317) 261-0500
Fax: (317) 261-0481
www.usatf.org

Triathlon Federation USA

3595 E. Fountain Blvd., Ste. F-1
Colorado Springs, CO 80910
Tel: (719) 597-9090
Fax: (719) 597-2121
E-mail:
USATriathlon@USATriathlon.org
www.USATriathlon.org

U.S. Volleyball Assn.

3595 E. Fountain Blvd., Ste. I-2
Colorado Springs, CO 80910
Tel: (719) 637-8300
Fax: (719) 597-6307
www.usavolleyball.org

United States Water Polo

Pan American Plaza, Ste. 520
201 South Capitol Ave.
Indianapolis, IN 46225
Tel: (317) 237-5599
Fax: (317) 237-5590
www.usawaterpolo.com

U.S. Weightlifting Fed.

One Olympic Plaza
Colorado Springs, CO 80909
Tel: (719) 578-4508
Fax: (719) 578-4741
www.usaweightlifting.org

USA Wrestling

6155 Lehman Drive
Colorado Springs, CO 80918
Tel: (719) 598-8181
Fax: (719) 598-9440
E-mail: usaw@concentric.net
www.usawrestling.org

The following addresses may also
be helpful:

Pan American Division USA Bowling

5301 South 76th Street
Greendale, WI 53129
Tel: (414) 421-9008
Fax: (414) 421-1194

American Amateur Racquetball Assn.

1685 West Uintah
Colorado Springs, CO 80904
Tel: (719) 635-5396
Fax: (719) 635-0685

U.S. Amateur Conf. of Roller Skating

P.O. Box 6579
Lincoln, NE 68506
Tel: (402) 483-7551
Fax: (402) 483-1465